CHALKWAYS OF SOUTH
AND SOUTH-EAST ENGLAND

By the same author

A CLIMBER IN THE WEST COUNTRY

CLIMBING AND WALKING IN
SOUTH-EAST ENGLAND

COASTAL PATHS OF THE SOUTH WEST

CHALKWAYS OF SOUTH AND SOUTH-EAST ENGLAND

by

EDWARD C. PYATT

maps compiled by Gillian Pyatt

DAVID & CHARLES
NEWTON ABBOT LONDON
NORTH POMFRET (VT) VANCOUVER

0 7153 6631 9

© EDWARD C. PYATT

Set in 11 on 13pt Times New Roman
and printed in Great Britain
by Latimer Trend & Company Ltd Plymouth
for David & Charles (Holdings) Limited
South Devon House Newton Abbot Devon

Published in the United States of America
by David & Charles Inc
North Pomfret Vermont 05053 USA

Published in Canada
by Douglas David & Charles Limited
3645 McKechnie Drive West Vancouver BC

CONTENTS

LIST OF ILLUSTRATIONS

PLATES

SKETCH MAPS

(All these are based upon the Ordnance Survey Map, with the sanction of the Controller of HM Stationery Office, Crown Copyright reserved)

Page

INTRODUCTION

ONE of the provisions of the National Parks and Access to the Countryside Act, 1949, was the setting up of a series of National Long Distance Paths. These were to enable the public to make extensive journeys on foot, or in some cases on horseback or bicycle, without passing along roads used by motor vehicles, the final aim being a continuous right-of-way throughout the whole length. The aim of this book is to describe the chalk areas of south and south-east England and the pattern of long-distance ridgeways there which are available to the walker. He may tramp them from end to end in expeditions which make considerable physical demands or, on the other hand, only accomplish a few miles at a time in day-long ambles or circular strolls. The central knot of chalkland, centred on Salisbury Plain and the Marlborough Downs, is first described, along with the subsidiary ridgeways which traverse these areas. Then the radiating ridgeways are treated one by one, always from the point of view of the walker travelling towards the central area. First comes the North Downs Way and the Inkpen Ridgeway which continues the line to Salisbury Plain; the South Downs Way follows with its extensions around the Weald to the North Downs Way and westwards towards Salisbury Plain. The Isle of Wight and South Dorset ridges are treated next. These used once to be continuous before the sea broke through into the Solent River. This is followed round to where it meets the Great Ridgeway coming up from the outposts of the chalk in East Devon. The Great Ridgeway itself is then described as far as Salisbury Plain. After a brief mention of Yorkshire and East Anglian chalk, the last trip to the central core area is taken via the Great Ridgeway, the Chiltern Hills and the Berkshire Downs on the line of the Ridgeway Path.

Though the rights-of-way have been established in the case of the Countryside Commission paths, there are not necessarily the same advantages in the other places described. There is very little wild open country and almost everywhere is in fact private property, even if it does not appear to be particularly cared for. Entry may be by usage or on sufferance, less frequently by right. In these cultivated and inhabited counties good relations with the local people are especially vital and the traveller, whatever his purpose in the countryside, must behave in a careful and responsible manner.

The three official paths—North Downs Way, South Downs Way and the Ridgeway Path—are illustrated by sketch plans on a scale of about 2½ miles to the inch; the remaining routes by strip sketch plans to the same scale but only half as wide. For each section of each path there is a general introduction with a summary of distances, followed by a route description and a local bibliography. There are appendices on topics likely to interest the traveller on the Paths, each with bibliographies indicating a range of further reading.

The plans are not of a scale large enough to replace the One Inch Ordnance Survey Map, which remains a must for the serious walker in the field. There is no guiding line here like the sea's edge on the cliff paths. Though the walker is rarely likely to be lost in a mist, a compass is quite useful, as the way is sometimes complicated and there is a lack of readily identifiable landmarks.

There are a number of methods for waymarking depending on the kind of country that the path is traversing. Either a signpost in oak with lettering raised or incised, or a low concrete plinth with the name of the route as part of the casting, will confirm that the traveller is on the right way. Another waymark at points where he might be in doubt is the acorn symbol, either a metal plaque attached to gateposts or fences, or a stencil marked on stone walls or boulders.

The going on these ridgeways can sometimes be monotonous and lacking in surprises, for the scenery sometimes changes very little over several miles of ground. They are not suitable therefore for the solo tramper, at least not for days on end, unless he indulges in some extra time-passing mental activity, such as composing poetry or solving problems in chess or mathematics. This, too, contrasts sharply with the coast paths, where the scenery is full of surprises.

No camping is possible on ridge tops and there is no potable water. In these days of site registration valley farms are unlikely to provide the casual facilities they once did. Sleeping out is a reasonable possibility when the weather is good, a bore if it is not. And the water problem is always there.

The on-and-on walker faces enough problems to modify the whole pattern of his journey. Towns and villages are invariably off to one side of the path rather than in gaps in the hills and a search for accommodation may lead far off the line of the route. The walker has to contend too with the modern attitude that a traveller without a car is little more than a tramp. These routes are not in popular holiday country and casual accommodation is notably less plentiful than in areas which are primarily touristy. Pre-planning of long distance routes and the necessary overnight halts sets too stern a requirement on weather, health, condition of feet etc and destroys the essential freedom of a tour. Most visitors will treat these ridgeways therefore in terms of day trips with approach by car, coach or train, the walk itself, depending on transport, either circular or extended to an alternative return point.

In the past one grew up to regard the open chalk downs as uncultivable, as indeed until World War II they were. Now it is usually only on the steep flanks that the characteristic turf cover is found; the tops are often widely cultivated and the modern vogue for huge fields can constitute a formidable hazard. It is little use to plan to see a hill-top fort or visit a downland summit between seed-time and harvest. It will be located out there in the middle as inaccessible to the well brought up country walker as if it were surrounded by crevassed glaciers. Prepare then for serious modifications of programme during the best months of the year. The lines of the official paths will always be open.

It is not necessary to recommend a technique for walking or the equipment to go with it. Shoes need to be stout; two widely differing pairs changed about provide restful variety. It may rain and blow, or the sun may shine brightly—appropriate counter-garments will be needed.

Finally, what do we gain from these chalk hills and their pathways? For everyone they have an important part to play in the development of a love of hill scenery. Here many an infant mountaineer is going to get his first impression of hills, of 'land set on land a little higher', and here he can keep fit subsequently in preparation for greater deeds on higher hills. The chalk downs are easily accessible heights in an area where very large numbers of people require outdoor recreation. Rising abruptly, on at least one side, from very flat plains, they make the most of their stature and, though certainly hills and emphatically not mountains, they attract by their form and their outline. The simple relics of early man contribute to the uniqueness, an open air archaeological museum of quite considerable proportions. Among high places they have a distinctive personality, so that the eminent mountaineer, Frank Smythe, could write of them: 'Height counts for little and it is the hill that matters. Low hills teach us that height, be it a mere two or three hundred feet, is something precious, something that quickens life to a nobler rhythm.'

The walking can be varied from the gentlest of gentle strolls to fiercely competitive exercises such as racing against the clock, taking all hills by their steepest ways, boosting up hills and racing down again or long-distance marathon walks. Everyone should be able to find a degree of activity appropriate to his needs.

MAPS

The Countryside Commission long-distance footpaths are illustrated by a series of maps on a scale of approximately 2½ miles to an inch, each covering a strip of country 16 miles by 10.

Other routes, which may in some cases follow roads rather than paths and on which there may not necessarily be rights-of-

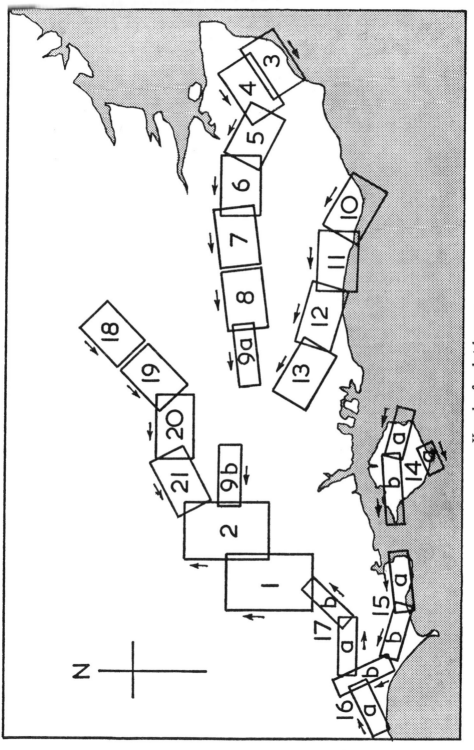

Key plan for sketch maps

way, even when there are paths, are shown on maps to the same scale, but covering strips of country 16 miles by 5.

The above are so oriented that the route towards Salisbury Plain passes up the page. The positions and orientations of the various sketch maps are shown on the preliminary key plan.

The central chalk areas of Salisbury Plain and the Marlborough Downs are illustrated on sketch maps to a scale of approximately 4 miles to an inch.

The following symbols are used on the maps:

KEY

▬▬▬▬▬	Countryside Commission long-distance footpath
•••••••••••	Great Ridgeway
•—•—•—•—•	Harrow Way
– – – – – –	Minor ways on Salisbury Plain
—•—•—•—	Minor ways on the Marlborough Downs
—— —— ——	Isle of Wight and South Dorset Ridgeways
—••—••—	Inkpen Ridgeway
▬▬▬▬▬	Imber Perimeter Footpath
ᴛᴛᴛᴛᴛᴛᴛᴛᴛ	Scarp edge
X	Principal antiquities

1

SALISBURY PLAIN—THE HEART OF THE CHALK COUNTRY

Stonehenge–Yarnbury Castle–Old Sarum–Salisbury
the Great Ridgeway–Warminster–Westbury–the Harrow Way
Amesbury–the Ox Drove Way–the Salisbury Way
Wilton–the Grovely Ridgeway

SALISBURY PLAIN was the centre of prehistoric England and here is found the biggest concentration of the remains of early man—camps, barrows, trackways, and so on, as well as the outstanding ritual centre of Stonehenge. Travellers to the far corners of the country used the chalk hill ridges radiating herefrom, which gave straightforward well-drained going above what were in those days the marshes and impenetrable woodlands of the valleys. Moreover from these commanding positions on the heights approaching enemies could be detected from afar and defied or evaded as seemed appropriate.

To understand the topography it is first necessary to notice the five rivers which meet in the neighbourhood of Salisbury. Of these the principal stream is the Avon which, rising in the Vale of Pewsey and breaking through the south wall by the same process as produced similar gaps in the North and South Downs, flows southwards to reach the sea at Christchurch. At Salisbury the Bourne joins from the north-east and the Nadder from the west, the latter having been joined already by the Wylye at Wilton. The Ebble enters the Avon, already swollen by the other three, some two miles further south. Salisbury Plain is the name given to the sector of chalk plateau between the Wylye and the Bourne and is bounded in the north by the Vale of Pewsey. There are ridges of chalk between the other rivers. South of the Ebble and sending a scarp down to the river is the Ox Drove ridge, which forms the edge of Cranborne Chase. Between here and the Nadder is

15

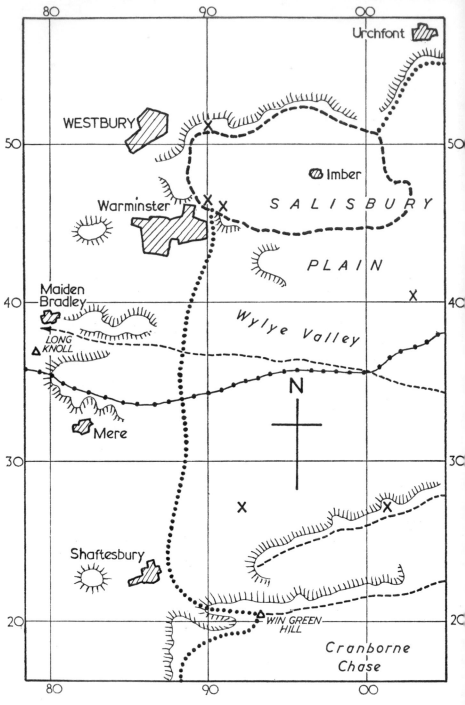

1 Salisbury Plain (West) and Cranborne Chase

another north-facing scarp carrying the Salisbury Way, while between the Nadder and the Wylye runs the Grovely Wood ridge.

The Plain is a rolling plateau of bare treeless slopes which has been likened to 'the petrified billows of some immense ocean'. For centuries it was sheep-grazing country but during the last three decades large areas have been put under cultivation. There is also a very considerable military presence. This began during the last century and with substantial increases during two world wars their holding now amounts to over 80,000 acres. Half of this is exclusive, but occasional use of the remainder is permitted to other interests. Any path in the area therefore may be subject to intermittent closure and the state of the game will have to be ascertained in advance before setting out on a route. We begin by looking at the principal antiquities, then at the lines of the early trackways, tackling finally the routes on the subsidiary chalk ridges listed above.

The circle at Stonehenge, two miles west of Amesbury between A303 and A344, the best preserved and the most striking in Britain, is a popular place of pilgrimage. Indeed so many of them come that it has been found impossible to maintain grass lawns in and around as the DOE usually does with its monuments. The great stones arise from a flattened area of bare, trodden earth. There is a fine example of a barbed-wire fence and the site is well provided (as indeed it has to be) with car parks, toilet facilities, kiosks and a tunnel beneath the road. Thus much of the awesomeness is lost among the summer crowds; but out of season, or even out of hours, the wonder of its setting and of its construction with primitive tools can still grip us.

The majority of the stones are local sarsens, great sandstone boulders left resting on the chalk after the strata containing them had eroded away. The so-called bluestones were brought, by method and route unknown, from the Prescelly Mountains in Pembrokeshire. The construction, including several rearrangements, took place between 1900 and 1400 BC. The underlying purpose, so long a subject of wild speculation, seems at last to have been deduced by computer-aided calculation. The circle is

B

in fact an astronomical calculating machine, which enabled the few who understood it to confound all the others who did not. It not only provided a calendar of the seasons, but it also made possible the prediction of future events in the Heavens such as eclipses—an excellent substitute for supernatural powers. As the *Shell Guide* puts it: 'It became from the first simple beginning to the final complex, an ingenious (if necessary) game, architects and priests contriving more and more astonishing observation posts through the stones for more and more surprising views of the sun and the moon.' That many of these stone circles had an astronomical purpose is revealed by Professor Thom in his recent book.

There are several fine camps on the Plain. Yarnbury Castle lies just off A303, 2 miles short of Deptford in the Wylye valley. Triple banks and ditches enclose an area of 28 acres; it is a tremendous work because the terrain makes almost no contribution to the heights of the banks or the depths of the ditches. The outer ditch is a mile long and the vallum is 50ft high. Battlesbury and Scratchbury Camps are just over a mile apart looking down on the Wylye close to Warminster. The former is 23 acres, with four ramparts on the downs side and steep slopes on the others; the latter is 40 acres and enclosed by banks and ditches. There are strip lynchets on Middle Hill halfway between. The Iron Age Bratton Castle (23 acres) is above Bratton village, 2 miles east of Westbury. On the scarp below, which faces north and west to the Somerset Avon, is the Westbury White Horse, created in 1778 and thus of reasonable antiquity. It replaced an even earlier model on the same site. Casterley Camp on the northern scarp of the Plain close to the Avon gap has only a single ditch and bank, but these enclose 60 acres. There are many other lesser remains scattered all over the Ordnance map, so that the traveller can hardly fail to discover them, provided that the military do not bar his way.

The outstanding antiquity of the big wedge of the Plain between the Avon and the Bourne is the Iron Age fort of Old Sarum, 2 miles north of Salisbury. The area is 27 acres, enclosed by two huge double banks and a ditch one mile in circumference.

The Romans captured the earthwork and founded Sorviodunum within the banks, an important centre from which roads radiated to Badbury Rings and Dorchester (Ackling Dyke), the Mendip Hills (along Grovely Wood ridge), Silchester (the Portway) and Winchester. In Norman times a cathedral and a castle were built in the enclosure, the nucleus of a thriving township. Later there were quarrels between the holy and the secular communities and the former began, around 1220, to construct Salisbury Cathedral in the valley below. Sarum Cathedral was demolished for the sake of its stonework; the castle too was a ruin by the fourteenth century. Little remains of either nowadays, but the great banks of the earlier works still endure. Much of the Plain to the north and east is under military domination with great modern camps at Tidworth and Bulford. The Bulford Kiwi, one of the largest of chalk figures, 420ft long and covering 1½ acres, was cut during the 1914–18 War. On the northern scarp above Pewsey an eighteenth-century horse was replaced as recently as 1937. The focal point of this area is the city of:

SALISBURY (SU12 to 16E, 28 to 32N). Road centre on A30, where A36, A338, A345, A354 and A360 meet. Main line railway station. E.C. Wed.

On the Avon at the confluence of the Nadder and the Bourne. The Cathedral was begun around 1220 when the ecclesiastics moved down from Old Sarum. The spire (404ft), the highest in England, is 2ft out of perpendicular because of great strains set up in the fabric. *See*: The Cathedral; the Close with King's House, College of Matrons and Mompesson House (National Trust); one of the four copies of the Magna Carta in the Cathedral library; dialless clock dating from 1326; many old houses, gates and bridges; St Thomas's, St Martin's and St Edmund's churches; museum; Guildhall; Council House. *Visit*: Racecourse (2½m W); Old Sarum earthwork (1½m N); Figsbury Ring (2½m NE); Clarendon Palace, scanty remains (2m E); Britford Saxon church and view of Salisbury across the water meadows (1½m SE) and Longford Castle nearby.

In its heyday Salisbury Plain was seamed with trackways, as a glance at the Ordnance map will confirm. Any one which is accessible will give interesting walking through almost prairie type terrain, disturbed most probably by noisy aeroplanes, tank exercises, gunfire, and so forth. We concern ourselves here mainly with the routes of the ancient long-distance ridgeways which may serve to interconnect the routes described in the later sections of this book.

The Great Ridgeway

This ancient cross-country route from Axmouth in Devon to Brandon and the Wash crossed the Plain diagonally from south-west to north-east. Climbing from the Wylye valley up alongside Battlesbury Camp, it followed the present minor road to Imber and on to St Joan à Gores Cross on A360 between Tilshead and West Lavington. This direct route is now more or less permanently closed by the military; Imber, apart from the church, has been almost completely destroyed in street-fighting practice. However, the problem has been tackled in a manner most acceptable under the circumstances by the creation of the Imber Perimeter Footpath, which is signposted and waymarked. Using this the range area can be passed either to the west and north or to the south and east as follows.

From Battlesbury Camp the route descends below Warminster Barracks and crossing Hill Down (694ft) runs north to Upton Cow Down above Westbury. Westbury Hill (755ft) with Bratton Castle and the White Horse is immediately beyond. Hippisley Cox believed that this was the actual line of the Great Ridgeway, though as we have seen more modern scholarship places it through Imber. We have passed above

WARMINSTER (ST86 to 88E, 44 & 45N). Access by A36 from Bath and Salisbury, by A362 from Frome and by A350 from Shaftesbury and Westbury. Railway station on branch line from Westbury to Salisbury. E.C. Wed.

In the upper reaches of the Wylye valley. *See*: church (fourteenth-century nave). *Visit*: Cley Hill (784ft) with summit camp (2½m W); Longleat House, safari park etc (4m WSW); Battlesbury and Scratchbury Camps (2m E).

WESTBURY (ST86/8750/51). Access by A350 from north and south and B3098 from east and west. Main line railway station. E.C. Wed.

See: Chained New Testament paraphrase by Erasmus in the church. *Visit*: Westbury Horse and Bratton Castle (2m E).

The route hugs the scarp edge first east, then north, then east again over Tinhead Hill (739ft), Stoke Hill (726ft) and Littleton Down to St Joan à Gores Cross on A360.

The southern alternative runs eastwards past Scratchbury Camp and Cotley Hill above Heytesbury. A series of ditches is passed with some antiquities inside the perimeter but Knock Castle earthwork outside it. We pass through Chitterne village and cross the downs to Tilshead, where there is a road to St Joan à Gores Cross, with the Perimeter Footpath as an alternative on its left.

Now we are back once again on the line of the Great Ridgeway. The route now skirts the Larkhill Range running north-eastwards by way of Urchfont Hill (712ft) and Redhorn Hill to Wilsford Hill, whence it descends past Broadbury Banks for a crossing of the Vale of Pewsey.

Instead of going north into the Vale, it is possible to continue above the scarp edge to Casterley Camp and so down to the valley of the Avon. On the far side is Pewsey Hill and Horse; we pass Giant's Grave long barrow and come to the shapely Easton Hill (over 750ft) topped by Easton Clump. The River Bourne is only a mile ahead and beyond it lies the Inkpen Ridgeway.

The Harrow Way

This route which has come from far-off Dover by the North

Downs to Farnham and onwards by routes now obscure, enters the Plain area at Cholderton on the Bourne. It has been largely obliterated by the modern road system. It passed to the north of:

AMESBURY (SU15/1641 and 1740). A303 now by-passes the town. Access from north and south by A345. Nearest station— Salisbury (7m). E.C. Wed.

In the Avon valley in the centre of the Plain halfway between Salisbury and the Vale of Pewsey; surrounded by military activities. *See*: church (part Norman); Amesbury Abbey (eighteenth century). *Visit*: Stonehenge (2m W); Woodhenge (1½m NE); Bulford Kiwi (3m NE).

Arrived at Stonehenge, the Way turned south-westwards by Druid's Lodge and Berwick St James to cross the Wylye at Steeple Langford.

The Ox Drove Way

Starting from Win Green Hill the Ox Drove runs for 10½ miles along the northern scarp edge of Cranborne Chase, looking down on the Ebble, and after a brief interlude on A354 continues for a further 5½ miles to Clearbury Ring near the junction of the Ebble and the Avon. Descending steeply from Win Green Hill, where the Great Ridgeway is left behind, the route is soon traversing a narrow ridge where deep valleys to the south have cut back towards the north-facing scarp. Winklebury Camp (9 acres) on a spur is not readily accessible in the cultivation season. The route stays back from the edge because of a series of large embayments in the scarp; the spurs—Marleycombe Hill (691ft), Knowle Hill (647ft) and Knighton Hill (595ft) are thus left on one side. Now we cross the line of the Roman road from Old Sarum to Badbury Rings and, descending, follow A354 for half a mile. To the south the ancient Grim's Ditch now serves in many places as the county boundary between Wiltshire and Hampshire. Beyond the line continues to Clearbury Ring, a single bank and ditch enclosure of 5 acres. On the far side of the river a scarp line leads on from Pepperbox Hill along Dean Hill towards Winchester.

The Salisbury Way

The Salisbury Way follows the ridges between the Ebble and Nadder rivers; A30 runs parallel to it on the north side on a shelf at the foot of the scarp. From the start at Harnham Hill in Salisbury to White Sheet Hill, where the trackway finally descends to join the modern road, are 13½ miles of rather monotonous going. This served as one of the main roads from Salisbury to Shaftesbury at least into the nineteenth century; a hard surface is still in evidence and the hedges, wildly overgrown, are placed wide apart. After passing the grandstand of the racecourse and crossing two minor roads we reach real hill country, but the trees and hedges often hide the distance. Below in the valley is:

WILTON (SU09/1030/31). Access by A30 from Salisbury and from the west and by A36 along the Wylye valley. Nearest station—Salisbury (2½m). E.C. Wed.

At the junction of the rivers Nadder and Wylye. Once capital of Wessex, now almost contiguous with Salisbury. Noted for carpet manufacture. *See*: Wilton House (Elizabethan and later) and gardens; carpet factory. *Visit*: Salisbury; Old Sarum; various National Trust properties at Dinton (5m W); Great Wishford church and village (3m NW).

We come to Chiselbury Camp (659ft) on a spur between Compton and Fovant Downs. A single bank enclosing 10 acres, it is completely inaccessible in the cultivation season. An interesting feature is the lengths of dyke on either side which are arranged in conjunction with the camp to block the whole width of the ridge top. Fovant Down has been the scene of a spate of modern chalk figure cutting, for within a short space there are several regimental badges, a map of Australia, a rising sun, and so on—subjects curious rather than enhancing. We cross Sutton Down (695ft), Middle Down (725ft) and White Sheet Hill (795ft) descending steeply at last to A30. A connection can be made with the Ox Drove from close to the summit of White Sheet Hill going down a spur to Berwick St John and climbing out again alongside Winklebury Camp to the ridge leading up to Win Green Hill and the Great Ridgeway.

In the Nadder valley a band of limestone and greensand runs from Shaftesbury towards Barford St Martin. Castle Ditches (1½ miles off A30) is another noteworthy earthwork. Tisbury has the largest barn in Britain—200ft long and 1,450sq yd of thatch on the roof. Three and a half miles away are the interesting ruins of fourteenth-century Wardour Castle. At Chilmark the Portland Stone for Salisbury Cathedral was quarried from underground caverns, which are there to this day. Unfortunately they are used as a bomb dump and no access is possible.

The Grovely Ridgeway

The chalk ridge between the valleys of the Nadder and the Wylye carries the extensive Grovely and Great Ridge Woods. There was an ancient ridgeway here and later the Romans took their road westbound from Old Sarum on much the same line. We leave the valley at Wilton and climb to the end of the ridge; both routes are inside the present-day woods, but there is a footpath line on the bare southern slopes which may be preferable. After 6 miles comes a minor road crossing close to Bilbury Rings, Churchend Ring and Hanging Langford Camp. At this point the Harrow Way comes in from the right up West Hill from Steeple Langford. A mile ahead the ways part again—the Ridgeway and the Romanroad reaching A303 by StocktonWood and continuing into Great Ridge Wood, the Harrow Way passing more southerly to join A303 at Chicklade Bottom. The Harrow Way now coincides with A303 for the next 5½ miles to Charnage Down, so that it is not of great use to the walker, who will be well advised to take the Ridgeway/Roman road route through Great Ridge

Wood, cross the Great Ridgeway (qv), here running north and south on the present A350, finally reaching Charnage Down by tracks and footpaths from Monkton Deverill. The Harrow Way now follows a fine section of chalk down to White Sheet Hill (802ft), where there is a hill fort as well as a Neolithic causewayed enclosure. Beyond we continue by Long Lane to Kilmington Common, thence a minor road continues the line to a point near King Alfred's Tower where we come to the end of the chalk. This is a folly in the grounds of Stourhead, one of the finest of National Trust properties, with magnificent gardens which should not be missed. The Harrow Way—no longer a walker's route and no longer on chalk—travels southwards to join the Great Ridgeway at Beaminster Down (westerly branch) or at Batcombe Hill (easterly branch).

The Roman road which we left near Monkton Deverill probably continued to Maiden Bradley and then by Whitham Friary and Shepton Mallet to the mines of Mendip. The early ridgeway may well have continued similarly though perhaps at a higher level, crossing (say) Brimsdown Hill (933ft) or Long Knoll (944ft), both of which carry antiquarian remains. The view from the latter extends from the English to the Bristol Channel.

From Wilton to the crossing of the Great Ridgeway (O.S. ST8836) is 14 miles; from there to King Alfred's Tower a further 11 thus makes 25 miles in all.

References
O.S. 1 inch Map Sheets 166, 167

2

THE MARLBOROUGH DOWNS

Marlborough–Silbury Hill–the Great Ridgeway
Hackpen Hill–the Outer Scarp Ridgeway–the Wansdyke Ridgeway
Devizes–Golden Ball Hill

THE Marlborough Downs extend the central chalk area northwards beyond the Vale of Pewsey. The centre for this area is:

MARLBOROUGH (SU18/1968/69). On A4. Access from the north
by A345 and from the south by A345 and A346. Nearest
stations—Pewsey (6m), Swindon (11½m). E.C. Wed.

On the River Kennet between Marlborough Downs and
Savernake Forest. There is a wide high street, very pleasant
now that M4 has reduced the through traffic. *See*: old houses
and inns. *Visit*: Savernake Forest (1m SE); Granham Hill
Horse (½m SW); Wansdyke (1½m SW); National Trust hold-
ings of sarsen covered downs at Piggle Dene and Lockeridge
Dene (3m W); Avebury, Silbury Hill and West Kennett Long
Barrow (5m W).

The Downs are similar to Salisbury Plain but without the over-
bearing military presence. The boundary in the south is the Vale
of Pewsey which, as we have said, is not a true river valley, but is
drained by the Salisbury Avon breaking through the southern
wall. The Downs are bounded in the west and round towards the
north by a series of scarps on the edge of the valley of the Somersetshire Avon. In the north-east a scarp edge springs from the Downs
to march eastwards for many a mile as the Berkshire Downs and
later the Chiltern Hills. We are now cut off from this by the M4
motorway which cuts across the ridge in the neighbourhood of
Liddington Hill before skirting the southern suburbs of Swindon.

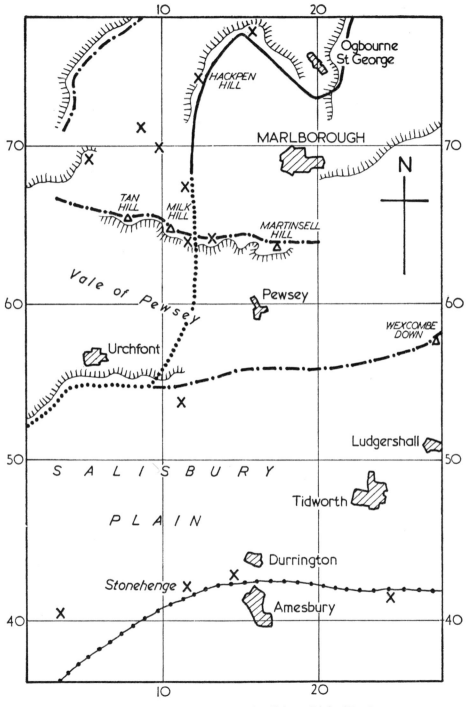

2 Marlborough Downs and Salisbury Plain (East)

For the present we set the eastern limit at the Og river which flows south to join the Kennet at Marlborough. The area thus defined divides into three.

The first is a ridge of high hills between the Vale of Pewsey and the upper Kennet valley (the line of A4), which includes Tan Hill and Milk Hill (both 964ft), the twin county summits of Wiltshire, and Martinsell Hill (950ft), one of the steepest and shapeliest of all chalk hills. The second is what might be called the inner downs, north and west of Marlborough, which end at a scarp at Hackpen Hill and Smeathe's Ridge. The third, the outer downs, is further north and west and ends at a second scarp by Compton Bassett, Clyffe Pypard and Wroughton.

Accepting the pre-eminence of Stonehenge, there is no doubt that the great stone circle at Avebury was the second important ritual centre of prehistoric Britain. Twenty-nine acres of level ground are enclosed within an earth bank a mile in circumference. Inside is a ditch once 50ft deep, lined on the inner edge by regularly placed large stones; formerly there were over a hundred of which only eighteen now remain. The stones are all local sarsens with no signs of working on them. The circle dates to about 1700 BC. The modern village of Avebury, where there is an interesting museum, stands within the ditch, much of the building material having come from the missing stones. It is possible too that some stones were transferred to contribute to the later stages of Stonehenge. From the south-east side an avenue of pairs of stones leads to the site of the Sanctuary, another stone circle, on Overton Hill beside A4. A mile further west on the same road, about one mile south of Avebury Circle, is Silbury Hill, 130ft high, 600ft across the base—a 'king-size' round barrow perhaps? It is a mystery monument for which no one knows the purpose. One and a quarter miles north-west of Avebury the camp on Windmill Hill, dating to 2500 BC, has given its name to a period of Neolithic culture. It is of the causewayed type which were used as social meeting places or dwellings rather than for defence. There are three lines of banks and ditches.

Of the 200 long barrows of various types remaining in this

country the majority are in Wessex. One of the finest, actually in fact a megalithic tomb, is preserved by the Department of the Environment at West Kennett, only half a mile south of A4 by Silbury Hill. A mile south-east there is another at East Kennett. Further south still is the impressive linear earthwork known as the Wansdyke which stretches with some interruptions from Morgan's Hill north of Devizes to the bounds of Savernake Forest. It was thrown up in the sixth century against invaders from the north.

White horses are plentiful—there are no less than six of them in this area. None is really ancient and none is earlier than the eighteenth century. On the north side of the Vale of Pewsey is the Alton Barnes Horse (nineteenth century), close to Marlborough there is one at Granham Hill south of A4 and another at Rockley beside the road to Wootton Bassett. The same road passes the Hackpen Hill Horse on the inner scarp and the Broadtown Horse further on carved on the outer scarp. Finally the Cherhill Horse is half a mile south of A4, 2 miles east of Calne. All this is horse country too in another sense for the Marlborough Downs, and the Lambourn Downs to the east, are one of the great racehorse training centres of the country. The horses are exercised over the Downs, so that it behoves walkers to behave circumspectly and to respect the rights of this important local industry.

The Great Ridgeway

The most important prehistoric route in this area is the Great Ridgeway which we left descending from Wilsford Hill on the northern edge of Salisbury Plain. Passing Broadbury Banks, it followed present-day footpaths through Wilsford to the minor road at Broad Street and on through Woodborough and Honey Street to Alton Barnes. Now a very impressive ridge line rises ahead with the Alton Barnes Horse prominent in a hollow below Walker's Hill. The Ridgeway line is slightly east of the present road but they go together through the gap between Walker's Hill (Adam's Grave long barrow) and Knap Hill (causewayed camp with single bank and ditch). At the summit the road bears right while the Ridgeway continues due north, crossing the Wansdyke and pressing on towards East Kennett. The East Kennett long barrow is passed on the left and we cross the infant Kennet to A4 at Overton Hill.

The route continues northwards on the far side up Avebury Down; this is now the line of the Countryside Commission's Ridgeway Path. The hillsides immediately to the east, Overton Down and Fyfield Down, are strewn with sarsen stones, fragmentary remains of newer geological beds which have otherwise been eroded away. They are often called Grey Wethers from their resemblance to sheep. The National Trust preserves two areas, Lockeridge Dene (south of A4) and Piggle Dene (north of it), which are typical. The scarp on our left gradually steepens and we reach Hackpen Hill (892ft) and a minor road crossing. The Hackpen Hill Horse is readily accessible from the car park at this point. The track continues contouring the hill for another mile and a half until we reach Barbury Castle, which has a double line of banks and ditches. The combe to the south has been identified as the site of an abandoned medieval village.

There are now two possible routes. The Great Ridgeway appears to have crossed the open ground to the north-east making direct for Liddington Castle on the opposite spur. The Ridgeway Path however stays on the hills. The scarp bends back southeastwards along Smeathe's Ridge to Ogbourne St George, where the Og can be crossed, and then runs north along the heavily ditched Whitefield Hill to Liddington Castle. This was once called Badbury after the even nearer village of that name. There are signs of extensive settlements around and this must have been an important centre of trackways.

Now the gigantic slash of the M4 motorway is before us, no greater incongruity can be imagined than the juxtaposition of these roads ancient and modern.

Wilsford Hill to Overton Hill is 9 miles; Overton Hill to Liddington Castle is another 10, while the route of the Ridgeway Path adds yet another 3½ miles.

The Outer Scarp Ridgeway

A walk on the outer scarp edge of the Downs can begin at Devizes by climbing up towards Roundway Hill. The small fort of Oliver's Castle is on a spur jutting westwards, while to the east of the track is the field of Roundway Down, where the Cavaliers defeated the Roundheads in 1643. After King's Play Hill (761ft) comes Morgan's Hill (853ft) with radio masts marking the beginning of the Wansdyke. On Cherhill Down above A4 there is a white horse (1780), the Lansdowne Monument erected to commemorate the birth of Edward VII and Oldbury Camp with double banks and ditches. Three and a half miles west is:

CALNE (ST9970/71, SU0070/71). On A4. Access from north and south by B3102. Nearest station—Chippenham (5½m). E.C. Wed.

Visit: Cherhill Horse and Oldbury Castle (3½m ESE); Morgan's Hill and the Wansdyke (3½m SSE).

After crossing A4 a way can be made as far as Wroughton on or near the scarp edge, the Broadtown Horse and Bincknoll Castle earthwork are passed en route. There are views across the valley of the Somersetshire Avon.

From Devizes to A4 is 9 miles and from A4 to Wroughton another 11.

The Wansdyke Ridgeway

This is one of the most spectacular routes on chalk, combining the rich antiquarian interest of the Wansdyke itself with some of the highest and finest of the chalk peaks. The Wansdyke was dug in the sixth century against invaders from the north; about eleven miles are reasonably well preserved hereabouts, but it did in fact originally stretch some sixty miles from Portishead on the Bristol Channel to Great Bedwyn in the Vale of Pewsey. In places

the banks are 25ft high so that it represents considerable move-
ment of earth. This ridgeway can easily be extended at the eastern
end by continuing on the Inkpen Ridgeway towards Basingstoke,
a route which would take in three county summits. We start from:

DEVIZES (SU00/0160/61). Access by A361 from the north-east,
A342 from the north-west, A361 from the west, A360 from
the south and A342 from the south-east. Nearest stations—
Chippenham (10½m), Pewsey (13m), Westbury (14m). E.C.
Wed.

See: old houses and inns; museum; Old Wool Hall
(eighteenth century); castle (nineteenth century); market cross.
Visit: magnificent staircase of locks (disused) on the Kennet–
Avon Canal (2m W); Wansdyke (4m NE); Etchilhampton
Hill (623ft) (1½m SE).

The Wansdyke is first met on Morgan's Hill, trending east-south-
east towards the big hills north of the Vale of Pewsey. In a mile
we reach A361 (Beckhampton to Devizes) and cross straight
ahead. The trackway parallels the bank and ditch for the next 2½
miles to Tan Hill (964ft), the summit of which rises just off to the
right. This shares the county summit of Wiltshire with Milk Hill
(same height) 1½ miles ahead. On the spur called Clifford's Hill
above the Vale of Pewsey is Rybury Camp. Trackway and defence
work continue in harness to Milk Hill, where the summit is again
away to the right. Cultivation right over the tops of many of
these hills makes peak-bagging impossible during the growing
season. Now the earthwork trends north of east while the trackway, seeking to follow the scarp, trends south of east. On the
latter we pass above the Alton Barnes Horse and come to the
Great Ridgeway just where it parts from the minor road on the col
between Walker's Hill and Knap Hill (857ft). The stature of
these hills gives them a commanding view over Salisbury Plain
on the opposite side of the Vale, where the average height is below

Page 33
Stonehenge, a
quarter of a
century ago

Page 34 Westbury Horse and Bratton Castle

800ft. The mound of Old Sarum and Salisbury Cathedral spire can be seen.

Half a mile ahead is Golden Ball Hill (879ft) followed by Huish Hill (856ft) leading down to A345, the Pewsey–Marlborough road. Martinsel Hill (950ft) is three quarters of a mile on. The long barrow—Giant's Grave—is sited on the spur above Oare; on the hill itself archaeologists have identified 'the site of a complete Neolithic settlement including dew ponds, a cattle compound, pit dwellings, a flint quarry, lynchetts, defence ditches and so on'. It is as near to a mountain as one can get on chalk. The descent on the far side leads to a minor road crossing and footpaths on to A346. On past the Kennet–Avon Canal and the Western Region main line, it is only a few miles now to the Inkpen Ridgeway.

There is no trackway along the remainder of the Wansdyke which passes through West Woods and thenceforward can be traced intermittently to the bounds of Savernake Forest, itself very attractive walking country of a widely contrasting type.

From Morgan's Hill to the Great Ridgeway crossing is 6 miles; on to A346 is another 8.

References
O.S. 1 inch Map Sheets 157, 167

C

3

THE NORTH DOWNS WAY
AND THE INKPEN RIDGEWAY

DOVER TO CHARING

Dover–Abbot's Cliff–Folkestone–Etchinghill–Stowting
Hastingleigh–Wye–Boughton Lees (or *Dover–Waldershare Park*
Shepherdswell–Barham Downs–Patrixbourne–Canterbury
Chilham–Boughton Lees)–Charing

LONG ago the North Downs extended across a land bridge to Cap Blanc Nez in France. The south facing scarp runs behind Folkestone before being cut off by the sea just beyond the Warren; exposures of chalk on the cliffs continue for the next ten miles to the other side of St Margaret's Bay. As at the start of the South Downs Way, so here also are there alternative routes, the one following the top of the steep cliff line to Folkestone and so reaching the top of the downland scarp, the alternative making a direct line through rural East Kent towards Canterbury. The former is the line of the ancient Harrow Way by which early man travelled from the short sea crossing at Dover along the spine of the Downs towards the centre of his world on Salisbury Plain. Much later pilgrims to the shrine of St Thomas at Canterbury often followed this ancient trackway coming from Winchester, or joining it elsewhere on the way, branching off finally through the Stour gap to their destination. The alternative route of the North Downs Way, mentioned above, aims to join this Pilgrims' Way at Canterbury.

From Dover to the *Valiant Sailor* by the cliffs is 5 miles, thenceforward it is 6 miles to Etchinghill, 4 more to Stowting and a further 6½ to Wye. Two and a half miles to Boughton Lees make this alternative sum to 24 miles. The other through the orchard country via Canterbury is somewhat further—7 miles

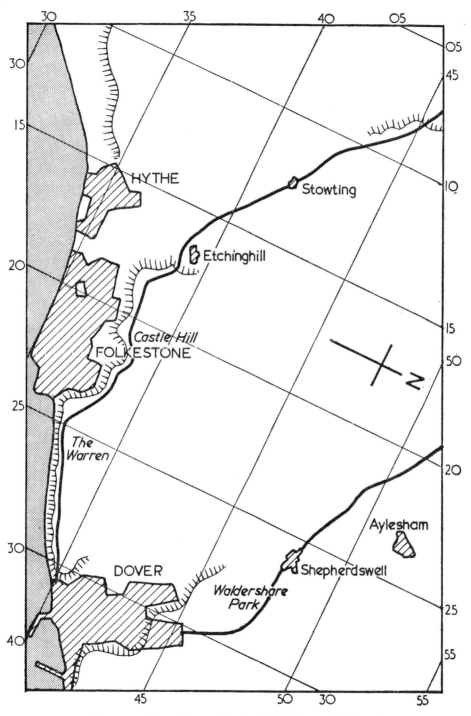

3   North Downs Way: Dover–Hastingleigh; Dover–Barham Downs

from Dover to Shepherdswell and 9½ from there to Canterbury; now through the Ouse gap it is some 12 miles to Boughton Lees— a total of 28½ miles. Boughton Lees to Charing is a further 4 miles, giving a shortest path distance for this section of 28 miles.

DOVER (around TR3141). Access by A2 from London, by A20 from Folkestone and A258 from Deal. Main line railway terminus. E.C. Wed.

Cross-channel port and resort with pebble beach at the mouth of the Dour, framed by the 'white cliffs'—Shakespeare Cliff to the west and South Foreland to the east. It dates back at least to Roman times. The remains of the Roman 'Pharos', which guided vessels from Gaul towards Richborough, still stands in the grounds of the castle. There was a settlement and a monastery in Saxon times, later the Normans built the magnificent castle which still dominates the town (*see*: Keep; Constable's Tower and other towers; underground works; the church of St Mary's-in-Castro and the Pharos). The present harbour, largely an artificial creation of breakwaters, began to grow in the reign of Henry VIII. It is now one of the largest man-made harbours in the world. *Visit*: Shakespeare Cliff (1m SW); South Foreland (2½m NE) and St Margaret's Bay (3m NE); Western Heights; Knight Templars' church.

The Way slopes up steeply from the town to the summit of Shakespeare Cliff, which is named for its mention in *King Lear*. Here the locals used to collect samphire, a thick-leaved herb, by lowering one of their number on a rope over the steep face. The layout of the bay and the harbours can be appreciated from here. A high cliff line leads westwards; the railway which hugs the coastline tunnels through Shakespeare Cliff, below which there was a colliery a hundred years ago, and again further on through Abbot's Cliff. Sometimes it may be necessary to go round by the road in this section, when the Lydden Spout range is in use.

Beyond Abbot's Cliff is the Warren (otherwise called 'Little Switzerland'), a classical landslip area at the cliff foot where there are interesting plants and fossils and some smugglers' caves. Some rock climbing was done hereabouts before the turn of the century by the famous A. F. Mummery. Borings for the Channel Tunnel were made here during the 1880s. A detour is probably worthwhile for the walker on the Way, for this is the last contact he will have with the coastline.

The Way crosses A20 close to the *Valiant Sailor* and follows a minor road up Creteway Down to A260. It is but a short distance to the summit of Sugar Loaf Hill; a so-called holy well lies below the northerly slopes. The path continues westwards by Round Hill to Castle Hill, on which is the erroneously named Caesar's Camp; the earthworks are in fact the remains of a motte-and-bailey castle of the eleventh or twelfth century. This is a fine viewpoint over Folkestone and the surrounding country; the cliffs of France can be seen on a clear day and the sandstone hills which reach the sea at Fairlight beyond Romney Marsh. Below us is:

FOLKESTONE (around TR2236). Access by A20 from Ashford and London, and from Dover, by A260 from Canterbury and A259 from the west along the coast. Main line railway station. E.C. Wed.

A fishing village of earlier times which grew into a resort during the nineteenth century. The railway came in 1843 and with it the construction of a cross-channel port alternative to Dover. *See*: fine promenade; harbour; the Warren landslip area (Little Switzerland) below the easterly cliffs; Sandgate Castle (not open to the public); Caesar's Camp (Norman earthworks). *Visit*: Hythe (parish church) (4m WSW); Saltwood Castle (4m W); the Royal Military Canal; Stutfall Castle (Roman) (6½m W); and martello towers.

Immediately to the west beyond Cherry Garden Hill the magical name Pilgrims' Way appears on the O.S. Map; any pilgrims here would have come from the continent. We follow minor roads and cart-tracks to Etchinghill diverging perhaps by way of the Battle-of-Britain airfield at Hawkinge and Paddlesworth, at 600ft the highest village in Kent. The actual line of the Way descends south-westwards from the hills and crosses the track of the disused railway to Combe Farm on B2065. Etchinghill lies in a gap between the main line of the scarp and the outliers—Point 795, Tolsford Hill and Summerhouse Hill.

The Way crosses Point 795 and descends beyond to Staple Farm. Footpaths north of Postling lead on to B2068, the line of the Roman Stone Street which ran from Stutfall Castle at Lympne (the Roman Lemanis) to Canterbury (which was Durovernum). The minor road to the south of these footpaths is labelled 'Pilgrims' Way' on the 1 inch O.S. Map. Stone Street is crossed (Map ref 135401) and the path continues until a minor road is joined by Cobb's Hill (Map ref 126412). By a minor road and then a cart-track we pass south of Stowting and north of Brabourne. The Way takes a track high on the hill, the parallel road at the foot of the slope is the Pilgrim's Way. Hastingleigh village is half a mile to the north. The route is complex taking a minor road for a short distance, then a footpath contouring the hill slopes above a series of small woods. We descend finally to a road junction half a mile north-east of Brook below Wye Downs. Now a footpath on the valley floor leads to Wye, a pleasant little town with old houses and Georgian mill-house. Crossing the railway the Way continues by footpath and minor road to Boughton Lees.

There is an entirely independent variant to this first part of the route. It bears no relation to the ancient trackways of the area, substituting for the sea-cliffs, and such scarp as there is, a rural route to the fine city of Canterbury, followed by the line of the Pilgrims' Way through the Stour gap to Boughton Lees.

Before leaving Dover once again, the fine walk on the chalk cliffs east of the town is noteworthy. Two and a half miles on the top of the 'white cliffs', starting with a plan view of the harbour and the car terminal, lead to the South Foreland with its light-house, a beacon for one of the busiest seas in the world. Soon afterwards we come to St Margaret's Bay, a shingle beach between chalk headlands, with St Margaret's-at-Cliffe inland above. Beyond on the cliffs is the Dover Patrol Memorial from the 1914–18 War: the cliffs finally peter out at Kingsdown. There are shingle beaches at Deal, where Julius Caesar landed, and Walmer and both places have fine examples of King Henry VIII coastal defence castles. Offshore beyond the anchorage called the Downs are the Goodwin Sands, remains of the ancient island of Loomea, now marked for shipping by a series of lightships.

The alternative route for the North Downs Way leaves Dover by the line of the old Roman road to Richborough. Track and footpath lead due northwards through Pineham to a road junction by Maydensole Farm, where we turn off westward through Waldershare Park to Shepherdswell (Sibertswold). To the north there are tumuli and a camp on Three Barrow Downs. This is the southern side of the Kentish coalfield. Barfreston close by to the north has a tiny Norman church.

The route along Barham Downs is complicated, parallel to but not using the A2 trunk road, formerly Watling Street. We turn away finally to Patrixbourne (interesting church with Norman features) and proceed through a countryside of orchards to Canterbury on the River Stour.

CANTERBURY (around TR1557). Access by A2 from London and from Dover, by A28 from Ashford and from Thanet, by A257 from Sandwich and A290 from Whitstable. Main line railway station. E.C. Thurs.

Now the chief cathedral city of the country, this site was occupied as long ago as the Iron Age. The cathedral was begun in the eleventh century and after witnessing the Becket murder in 1170 became a shrine of pilgrimage ('from every shires ende of Engelond, to Caunterbury they wende, the holy blisful

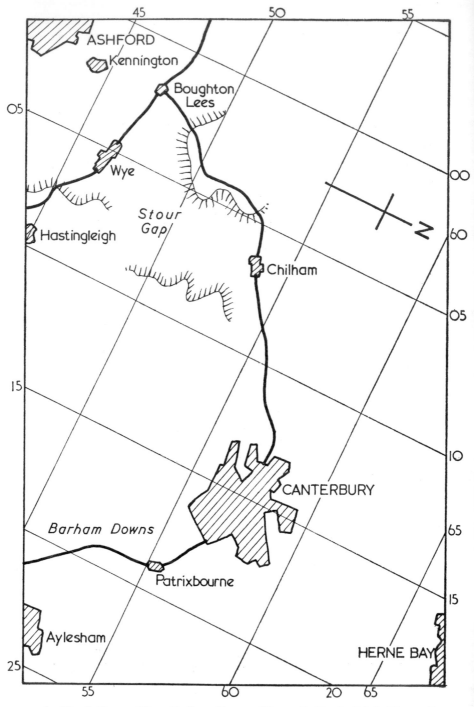

4 North Downs Way: Barham Downs–Westwell; Hastingleigh–Westwell

martir for to seke . . .', as Geoffrey Chaucer tells us). The cathedral and the many other interesting features make the city an outstanding tourist attraction. *See also*: West Gate built in 1380; St Thomas's Hospital (Norman hall); museum; remains of Norman castle ('one of the most elaborately planned hall-keeps in the country'); St Augustine's Abbey and College; St Martin's church (the oldest used church in England, dating back before St Augustine); St Mildred's church; many old houses. *Visit*: Harbledown (St Nicholas's church and Bigbury Wood earthwork) (2m W); Whitstable (sand and shingle beach, famous for oysters; the railway between Whitstable and Canterbury was the first passenger line in this country) (5½m NNW).

Before proceeding with the Way, we can turn aside here to look at another small area of chalk on the Isle of Thanet. The Stour flows north-eastwards from Canterbury finally reaching the sea at Pegwell Bay between Sandwich and Ramsgate. The last few miles of its course follow the Wantsum Channel which in Roman times separated Thanet from the remainder of Kent. This was guarded by massive forts at either end. In the north, Reculver (Regulbium) has been partially destroyed by the sea; the ruins of a Saxon church, the twin towers of which were preserved because of their importance as a seamark, now characterise the site, which otherwise might become entirely obliterated by cara-vans. Richborough (Ritupiae) at the eastern end still retains some of the massive original walls of the fort, as Leland wrote—'very hye, thykke, stronge and wel embateled'; there are town walls also, an amphitheatre and a museum.

The Isle of Thanet reaches 180ft. It is ringed with chalk cliffs on the seaward sides, now much modified by promenades, houses, walls and sea defences—as well as the amenities of a continuous row of seaside resorts—Ramsgate, Broadstairs, Margate, Westgate and Birchington. The chalk sea-stacks at the last, a famous coastal feature, were blasted away to make a promenade.

There is a natural cave still, 280ft long, the so-called Smugglers' Cave at Kingsgate, as well as other lesser ones.

The Way leaves Canterbury by West Gate to Harbledown and soon it is orchard country once again. The path climbs eastwards to Bigbury Wood camp, an early Iron Age fort now mostly on private land, where Caesar defeated the Britons in 54 BC, and on by minor roads to Chartham Hatch. Two miles ahead is Chilham, a pretty village with some fine old houses and a notable castle with a keep of unusual octagonal design constructed by Henry II. To the south-west on Jullieberrie Down is the long barrow known as Jullieberrie's Grave (144ft long). The Way skirts Chilham and Godmersham Parks and comes to Boughton Lees by way of Soakham Downs to rejoin the route described above.

We now enter Eastwell Park, passing close to Eastwell Lake and the ruins of a church. The line is on, or very close to, the Pilgrims' Way and continues along the scarp edge past Westwell (fourteenth-century church) to A252. Half a mile away in the valley is Charing which has some old houses and a gateway and other remains of an Archiepiscopal Palace.

References
O.S. 1 inch Map Sheets 173, 172
O.S. 2½ inch Map Sheets TR34, 23, 13, 14, 04, TQ94 for shorter (Folkestone) route and TR34, 24, 25, 15, 05, 04 for longer (Canterbury) route

CHARING TO WROTHAM

Charing–Lenham–Harrietsham–Leeds–Hollingbourne
Detling–Kit's Coty House–Burham–Rochester Bridge
Upper Halling–Trottiscliffe–Wrotham

The outstanding feature of this section is the Medway Gap, which, as befits a more considerable river, is broader than the others of the North Downs. The gap marks the only major change of direction in the whole length of these hills, which have followed an almost straight line somewhat west of north-west from Dover and hereafter run equally straight somewhat south of west all the way to Farnham at the far end of Surrey. The proximity of several large towns—Maidstone to the south and Rochester, Chatham and Gillingham to the north—has led to a greater degree of industrialisation, so that for some miles the cement works and the paper mills are inescapable.

The section between Charing and Detling was described by Belloc as 'a type of what the primitive wayfarers intended when the conditions offered them for their journey were such as they would have chosen out of all . . . well-drained, uninterrupted by combes or promontories, the range of hills exactly even'. Thus ran the Harrow Way 'commanding a sufficient view of what is below and of what lies before'. The average height of the hills increases as we move west; here, east of Maidstone, they attain only 600–650ft, 700ft is reached for the first time by Wrotham and 800ft only near the county's end above Westerham.

From Charing to Lenham is 4½ miles, a further 4 miles lead to Hollingbourne, whence it is 5 miles to Detling. There are alternative ways of crossing the Medway Gap; the official route of the North Downs Way leads by way of Burham (5 miles) to cross the Medway at Rochester Bridge, another 3½ miles. Now it is 3½ miles to Upper Halling, 4½ miles on to Trottiscliffe and 2½ more to Wrotham—a total for the section of 33 miles.

After crossing A252 close to Charing the North Downs Way follows a minor road, parallel to and sometimes very close to A20, which is lower down the slope with the main line railway to Dover beyond. Here we are exactly on the Pilgrims' Way also. Four and a half miles lead to Lenham which is fortunate in being by-passed by A20. There is an old church, a tithe barn and some interesting houses, with the Old Market House in the centre of the square. The next village—Harrietsham, less lucky—is bisected by A20. Southwards beyond the River Len the Lower Greensand hills start to emerge as a ridge parallel to our own. From Boughton Malherbe church there is a fine view over the Weald to the

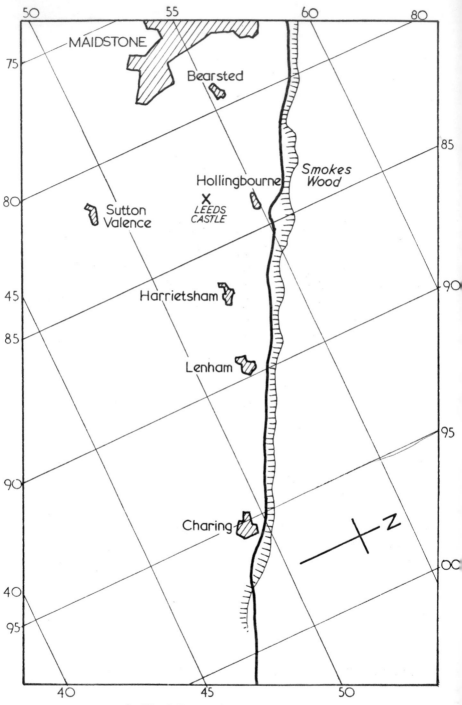

5　North Downs Way: Westwell–Boxley

Fairlight Hills close to Hastings. Hereabouts A20 and the railway change places, but our line on the scarp slope rolls straight on for a further 2 miles to B2163 above Hollingbourne (a pleasant village with a Tudor manor-house).

After B2163 the Pilgrims' Way and the North Downs Way part company, the former continuing ahead by more trackway, the latter striking northward as a path. After 500yd the path turns to the north-west and runs parallel to the Pilgrims' Way even higher up the slope. Soon we reach a footpath crossing. If this be followed on the right towards Hucking, we come in half a mile—just inside Smokes Wood—to a fine example of a dene-hole, a countryside feature essentially Kentish, though there are indeed a few also in Essex.

Dene-holes are vertical shafts, in places up to 80ft deep, found on the dip slope of the North Downs, which penetrate the over-lying sands into the chalk strata. Sometimes there are regular chambers at the foot, but never tunnels. Of the numerous theories regarding their origin the most plausible seems to be that they served as chalk mines, providing material to lighten heavy soils. Dene-holes are most plentiful close to London in the neighbourhood of Bexleyheath, Crayford and Orpington, though there are isolated examples widespread, even right back to Dover. They cannot be explored without suitable caving tackle and the passing walker can do no more than look from the surface. The hole in Smokes Wood is 8ft in diameter and after running through 8ft of sand penetrates 39ft into the chalk; there are three chambers (possibly four) at the foot.

In the valley beyond Hollingbourne and Eyhorn Street the Maidstone By-pass can be seen terminating on A20. The construction of this new road destroyed, unfortunately, a magnificent and complex series of man-made caves in sandstone, in which the notable spelaeologists, Baker and Bonner, were once hopelessly lost for several hours. South of the junction is the village of Leeds with the eighteenth-century Battle Hall and a church with an eleventh-century tower. Close by is the striking Leeds Castle, built on two islands in a lake formed by damming the River Len.

The original castle was constructed in the twelfth century, but much of the present building is only 150 years or so old. It can be seen from the road or from a footpath through the park, but there is only occasional admission.

Meanwhile on the Downs the pattern is maintained—the North Downs Way a footpath highest on the slope, then a minor road marking the line of the Pilgrims' Way, lower still the Maidstone By-pass and the railway. On the hill above the tiny village of Thurnham are the sparse remains of a Norman castle with some indication of a keep, and a fine view. The path converges on A249, which is crossed at Detling (church, part Norman). Some two miles south-west is:

MAIDSTONE (TQ75/7654/55/56). County town of Kent. Important road centre on A20, now by-passed by M20 motorway. Important rail centre also. E.C. Wed.

On the River Medway, below the Downs on the south side of the Medway Gap. *See*: Archbishop's Palace (Elizabethan); ancient tithe barn, now a museum; Chillington Manor (Elizabethan), now Museum and Art gallery. *Visit*: Fifteenth-century Wool House (National Trust) at Loose (2m S); Boughton Monchelsea Place (Elizabethan) (4½m S), archae-ological remains have been found in a cave nearby; cave in Kentish Rag in Senacre Wood (2m SE); slight remains of a castle at Sutton Valence (5m SE); Stoneacre House (late fifteenth century) at Otham (3m SE); Leeds Castle (5m ESE); village green at Bearsted (2m E) where Wat Tyler's forces assembled in 1381; Boxley Abbey remains (2m N); remains of long barrow, Kit's Coty House (3½m NNW); Allington Castle (1½m NW), a Norman castle much restored during the early part of this century, well seen from the tow-path; Aylesford (2½m NW), ancient bridge and the Friary; West Malling (4½m WNW), St Mary's Abbey and very decayed ruins of a castle keep and gatehouse; Yalding (5m SW), pleasant village among hop-gardens with ancient bridge.

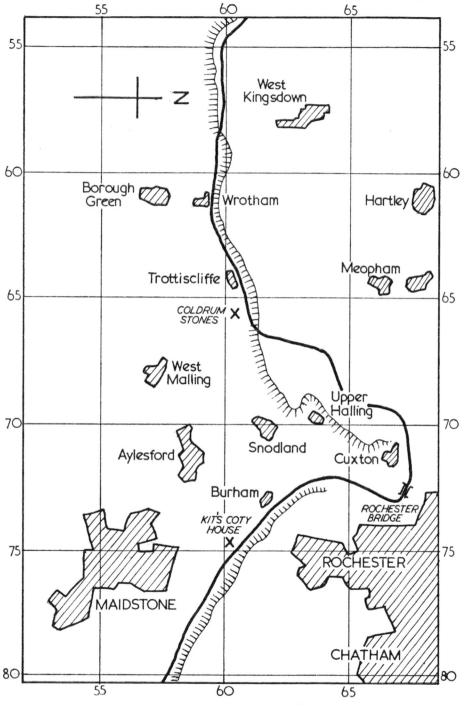

6 North Downs Way: Boxley–Kemsing

From A249 the path runs north a short way before turning north-west once again along the scarp. Here we are above a wood with the Pilgrims' Way parallel below it. In one and a half miles we arrive above Boxley, a pleasant village with attractive church and green and a few remains of an abbey. The path continues in and out of woods, the alignment chosen to stay away from the M2 motorway, to A229 which was the Roman road from Maidstone to Rochester. Not quite a mile to the south and almost on the line of the more ancient Way is Kit's Coty House, a celebrated anti-quity—the remains of a megalithic tomb; nearby are the so-called Countless Stones.

The crossing of the Medway was a serious undertaking for the early traveller and it remains for different reasons an obstacle even today. It seems probable that the prehistoric route crossed the river by a ford at Snodland and this, concluded Belloc, was also the line of the Pilgrims' Way. There is no bridge at Snodland, so the North Downs Way hugs the scarp edge towards the north, utilises the Medway Bridge built for the motorway and then on the far side climbs back on to the hills as soon as possible. In view of the heavy industrialisation of the valley it might perhaps be better to cross as expeditiously as possible, say by descending alongside Kit's Coty House, crossing the river at Aylesford and, after a short section of A20, following a line of footpaths through Leybourne and Birling back to the Pilgrims' Way and the Downs. There is no perfect solution.

From the A229 crossing the North Downs Way continues by a minor road on top of the scarp. In less than a mile we pass above Burham village with an old manor-house and a flint-and-stone church; in the background are the factories. The road becomes a track swinging north, then east, to come to the M2 motorway. In a mile we reach and cross the Medway Bridge. Only a mile and a half away is:

ROCHESTER (TQ72/7368/69) with CHATHAM, GILLINGHAM and STROOD contiguous. A conurbation on A2 (the Roman Watling

Page 51   Hackpen Hill, looking towards Avebury

Page 52   The Wansdyke, looking to Morgan's Hill

Street), where this crosses the Medway. Main line railway stations. E.C. Wed.

Heavily industrialised port and naval dockyard towns. There are numerous associations with Charles Dickens. Rochester, closest to the crossing, has the longest history. It was Roman Durobrivae and Saxon Hrofe-caestre. There is a fine Norman cathedral and a splendid example of a Norman square keep, substantial reminder of the former castle. *See also*: numerous old houses and churches, also museum in Rochester. *Visit*: remains of twelfth-century Temple Manor ($\frac{1}{2}$m S of Strood); Cooling Castle (gateway only) and the marshes of *Great Expectations* (4m N); Owletts (seventeenth-century house) at Cobham (4m W).

On the west bank A228 runs parallel to the river. After a few hundred yards it is possible to break away to the south-west by a footpath alongside Merrals Shaw. Cuxton village is close by. For the next few miles the terrain is complex and the line somewhat indirect. The railway is crossed by a footbridge north of Court Lodge, whence a path leads to the minor road west of Cuxton. Another path beyond leads to Upper Bush and then directly south through North Wood across to Wingate Wood, where we are on the top of the North Downs scarp once again. Below in the valley are Upper Halling, Halling and Snodland with quarries, cement works, and so on. For some distance now the route lies mainly in woods, passing close to Householders' Wood, Great Buckland and Holly Hill to reach at Holly Hill Lodge a minor road which has climbed the scarp steeply from Snodland.

On the opposite side we follow a path which descends the scarp to join the line of the Pilgrims' Way, here unmistakably identifiable as a line of trackways and paths along the valley below the steepest part of the hill. Eventually the Pilgrims' Way becomes a minor road, but the North Downs Way cunningly avoids this by a parallel footpath at a slightly higher level.

D

South now is the village of Trottiscliffe with, half a mile east, an interesting church and the remains of a Bishop's palace, and a further half a mile east the Coldrum Stones (National Trust), the remains of another megalithic tomb. Further off, close to A20, is Addington village with a church (part thirteenth century) on a mound, sarsen stones and remains of further tombs. Beyond A20 is Offham village, which has on the green the only example in England of a quintain, apparatus for a medieval tilting sport which died out in the eighteenth century. Here we are rising towards the Lower Greensand ridge, clothed hereabouts with the very extensive Mereworth Woods.

The route continues below the woods on the scarp face, the hills above reach 700ft for the first time. Near Wrotham we rejoin the Pilgrims' Way soon crossing the busy A20 trunk road, which here crosses the scarp. Just beyond is:

WROTHAM (TQ61/6259). On A227, just off A20. Main line railway station at Borough Green (1m S). E.C. Wed.

There is 'the most famous vista in the county' from A20 at the top of the scarp; it will invariably have to be shared. *Visit*: Oldbury Hill (3m SE); Ightham Mote (3½m SSE); Coldrum Stones (2½m ENE).

References
O.S. 1 inch Map Sheets 171, 172
O.S. 2½ inch Map Sheets TQ65, 66, 75, 76, 85, 94, 95

WROTHAM TO REIGATE

Wrotham–Otford–Sevenoaks–Chevening–Betsom's Hill
Westerham–Titsey–Oxted–Godstone Caves–Merstham
Redhill–Reigate

This section includes the county summit of Kent, which lies on the Downs almost at the Kent/Surrey border. Hereabouts was the major scene of the one-time hearthstone mining, which has left the countryside honeycombed with man-made caverns in various stages of delapidation. Down on the dip slope is the biggest concentration of those mysterious dene-holes, the chalk mines which we encountered in the previous section. It is popular day-walking country for Londoners at weekends with plenty of communications.

From Wrotham to Otford is 6 miles, a further 3½ lead to Chevening and 5 miles on from there completes the traverse of Kent. Now in Surrey, 6 miles lead to Godstone Caves, a further 5 bring us to Merstham and 2 finally to the crossing of A217 on Reigate Hill. The total for this section is thus 27½ miles.

At the A20 crossing the North Downs Way is exactly on the line of the Pilgrims' Way. After 300yd on a minor road the route continues straight ahead by trackway at around 450ft below the steepest part of the scarp, which here reaches 750ft. We cross one minor road and in 1½ miles come to another at a right-angled turn. Here the Pilgrims' Way continues ahead by a minor road while the North Downs Way turns north on a footpath, and soon afterwards west again at a higher level. St Clere down below is a red brick manor-house of the seventeenth century with a wealth of chimneys. Two more minor roads are crossed, the second close to Cotman's Ash House. A complex area of terrain leads on to the road by Otford Court. Below in the valley is Kemsing village (main line railway station; Youth Hostel), which lies directly on the line of the Pilgrims' Way. From the road junction by Point 669 a footpath descends the shoulder of the hill to:

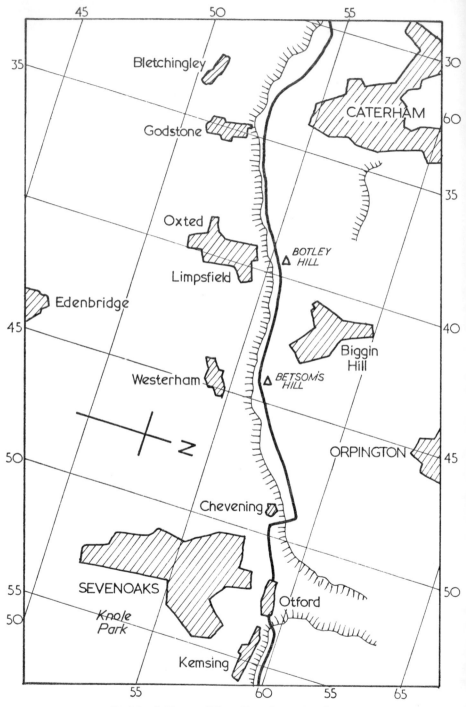

7 North Downs Way: Kemsing–Merstham

OTFORD (TQ52/5358/59). Access by A225. Main line railway station. Youth Hostel at Kemsing (1½m E). E.C. Wed.

Village in the Darent Gap at the foot of the scarp. *See*: ruins of palace of the Archbishop of Canterbury; Roman villa site.

In this last section we have been walking parallel to an interesting stretch of the hills of Lower Greensand, which would be well worthy of a detour. Ightham Mote, some four miles south of St Clere, is a well-known moated manor-house, part dating to the fourteenth century, sometimes open to the public. There is a considerable Iron Age fort in the woods on Oldbury Hill above Ightham village; close by is an outstanding antiquity—rock shelters from Palaeolithic times (that is more than 100,000 years BC). Flint implements were found here similar to those from Le Moustier cave in France and from other sites in the Dordogne.

At Otford the Darent Gap is some two miles wide. After a short section of A225, we walk through the village and eventually turn south-west. The railway is crossed by a footbridge and A21 reached below the steeper part of Polhill. Only 2 miles south is:

SEVENOAKS (TQ51 to 53E, 54 to 56N). Access by A21 and A225 from the north, A21 from the south, A25 from east and west. Main line railway station. E.C. Wed.

On the northern dip slopes of the Lower Greensand hills facing across to the Downs and the Darent gap. Knole House, begun in the mid-fifteenth century and extended in the early seventeenth, is a major attraction. There are 1,000 acres of parkland. *See also*: various old houses, including the seventeenth-century Chantry House.

From A21 the route crosses the quadrilateral of roads in O.S. Square 5058 to the crossroads in the western corner. The route follows the left-hand road for half a mile and then turns north-west towards Knockholt Pound skirting Chevening Park (gardens sometimes open to the public). We continue along the northern edge of the Park, eventually joining a line of minor roads beyond running along the foot of the scarp. The North Downs Way climbs higher up the scarp, which here is not particularly steep, towards the Kent/Greater London boundary, but turns short of this and stays in Kent to cross A233 at the top of Westerham Hill, immediately north of Betsom's Hill Farm. A mile to the south is:

WESTERHAM (TQ4453/54). On A25. Access by A233 from the north and B2026 from the south. Nearest station—Sevenoaks (5½m). E.C. Wed.

General Wolfe was born here, statue in the main street, museum in Quebec House (National Trust). *Visit*: Betsom's Hill (1½m NW); Chartwell—the home of Sir Winston Churchill (2m S); Squerryes Court (house, sixteenth century and later, with Iron Age camp in the grounds) (1m SW); sandstone hills to the south with a small cave on Hosey Common.

Westerham lies in the so-called Vale of Homesdale, a valley formed between the outcrops of chalk and Lower Greensand by the more rapid erosion of Upper Greensand and Gault clay. To the south the Lower Greensand reaches for the first time a height comparable with that of the chalk. There is a sizeable block of country above 700ft around Crockham Hill, Ide Hill and Toys Hill, the latter reaching a summit in excess of 800ft.

After we have crossed A233, Betsom's Hill (824ft) is immediately to the north. This is the county summit of Kent, marked on the 2½ inch O.S. Map as 'Fort Westerham (disused)'. Onwards we soon pass over into Surrey, continuing towards Tatsfield church which rises just off B2024. Titsey Hill on B269 is crossed on the scarp above Titsey village. At the top the North Downs reach the highest point of their whole length—875ft beside the road leading south-west from the road junction at Botley Hill. Presumably it would not be too wrong to assign the name to the hill. Further along, this road runs above a large chalk quarry, looking out on an extensive view.

The North Downs Way travels parallel to this road on the lower side of Titsey Plantation by footpaths which are always higher than the Pilgrims' Way, also parallel but further downhill. We pass below the large quarry and cross the Oxted Line above the southern end of Oxted Tunnel. Oxted village (old houses and church; station on branch line from East Croydon to Groombridge and East Grinstead) is only a mile away on A25; contiguous to the east is Limpsfield. The route now traverses the National Trust holding of Hanging Wood on Tandridge Hill and, crossing two more minor roads, reaches A22 between Godstone and Caterham.

At this point we are vertically above a very extensive series of man-made caves, which are actually an abandoned hearthstone mine. This rock, also called firestone, one of the component beds of the Upper Greensand, was used in bygone days, before transport became adequate to move better materials from further away, as a building stone (parts of Westminster Abbey, Windsor Castle, Hampton Court, Croydon almshouses and Town Hall, numerous churches, and so on). Later it was applied to the bases and sides of fire-places, and used for whitening door-steps. Quarrying was accomplished by driving tunnels into the hill along the required stratum; the material is soft at first but hardens on exposure. No mining operations have been carried out here since the 1914–18 War, though round the turn of the century dozens of men were employed on the various sites— here and at Gatton, Merstham, Betchworth and Colley Hill, Reigate. Work indeed continued at the last in a minor way until 1960.

Entrances appear and disappear with the passing of time, but it is still possible to find a way into these particular caves for anyone who is interested. While some care is needed there is no reason to suppose that this would involve any considerable danger. Protective headgear, lights and some commonsense are the prime needs of the would-be explorer. While the passing walker may well believe himself adequately endowed with the last, he is unlikely to be carrying either of the others. The passages are of uniform height and width and there is little or no resemblance to natural caves. There have been a number of projected uses in recent years but all are now derelict; a study of their history would be a rewarding project, but there would be complications because all the historical records fail to distinguish between open-cast working and tunnels, referring to them indiscriminately as 'quarries'.

Crossing A22 by a bridleway-bridge, the route follows a minor road at first, but where this turns north, there is a footpath southwards. The next mile or so, passing Fosterdown Fort on the way, is mostly in woods. The path runs parallel to, and south of, the minor road which skirts Gravelly Hill; then at a crossroads the minor road straight ahead is followed along White Hill. Now we are on the top of the Downs once again at 700ft or so and almost on the outskirts of Caterham.

Southwards below the scarp on A25 is the village of Bletchingley, with a wide main street and some very broken remains of a castle of the late twelfth century. Four miles further on are the notable windmills at Outwood—the post mill, which is well preserved, dates from the seventeenth century; the nearby smock mill unfortunately fell down in 1960.

Soon the route turns from north-west to west and passes a radio station and Point 723 to another minor road. The National Trust holding known as Six Brothers' Field is close by to the north. The track ahead leads to Tollsworth Manor Youth Hostel, but the Way turns south-west over Ockley Hill and after crossing M23 by an underpass comes to Merstham. Under foot hereabouts were the passages of the old hearthstone mine, now obliterated by the motorway. Some caving groups were allowed to explore here during the last two decades and surveys and maps were made.

After 300yd southwards on A23 it is possible to break away to the west and to climb out of Merstham through the grounds of Gatton Hall. In half a mile we cross the site of Gatton hearthstone mine, another which has been explored within the last few years. The route stays south of the minor road from Merstham to Reigate Hill and we come eventually through National Trust land to A217 on the hill top without having to touch on it. South now are:

REIGATE and REDHILL (TQE25 to 28, N48 to 51). Contiguous towns on A25. Access from north and south to Redhill by A23 and to Reigate by A217. Main line railway station (Brighton Line) at Redhill. Railway station at Reigate on cross country line running east and west. E.C. Wed.

Reigate is the older town, Redhill grew up round the railway in the last century. There is no gap in the Downs here, the main roads climb over, the railway from the north comes by Merstham Tunnel. Reigate has slight remains of a Norman castle with a show cave in the sandstone below. In Reigate, *see also*: Reigate Priory; Parish church; old houses, notable market house. *Visit*: Windmills at Outwood ($3\frac{1}{2}$m SE); Reigate and Colley Hills (2m NW); Windmill on Reigate Heath (2m W).

References
O.S. 1 inch Map Sheets 170, 171
O.S. $2\frac{1}{2}$ inch Map Sheets TQ25, 35, 45, 55, 65

REIGATE TO FARNHAM AND BEYOND

Reigate–Betchworth Chalk Pits–Box Hill–River Mole
(Dorking)–Newlands Corner–St Martha's Church
River Wey (Guildford)–Puttenham–Farnham
Extensions to the South Downs, to the Inkpen Ridgeway and to
Salisbury Plain (the Harrow Way)

This section of the North Downs is the Londoner's walking country, communications are good, footpaths plentiful and weekends are always likely to see walkers out on the roads and tracks. Equally it is popular motoring country; all road access points have large car parks, will often be crowded and hardly ever deserted. In fact escape from people is more likely to be achieved in the rural terrain at the foot of the scarp than on the scenically popular hill slopes.

This part of the North Downs Way is seldom likely to be walked as a continuous expedition. Accommodation, except of the most expensive variety, will be limited, for there is nothing like the bed-and-breakfast tradition of, say, the West Country. The ground will be covered almost invariably in day-long sections.

These hills are not rich in antiquities and are built over more than all other chalk downlands. The clay-with-flints, lying on top of the chalk and stretching up to the scarp edge, favours the growth of woodlands in place of the typical downland landscape of bare chalk. Though sometimes cutting off the distant view, it is possible that this leads to a more varied landscape. But it is not typical of what we expect from chalk—quite different from the eastern end of the South Downs or the downs of Berkshire and Wiltshire. Nearness to London is quite sufficient to account for its popularity—for popular it certainly is.

Reigate Hill (A217) to the Dorking Gap is 7 miles, on to Newlands Corner another 9 miles and thence to the Wey crossing 4 miles. Now it is 4 miles to Puttenham and a further 6½ miles to the end of the North Downs Way at Farnham; a total of 30½ miles. The routes onwards to the west are of little use to the walker, but it is in fact about 26 miles from here by way of Ellisfield Camp to Cottington's Hill on the Inkpen Ridgeway.

The North Downs Way and the Pilgrims' Way cross A217 at the top of Reigate Hill by a bridleway-bridge, as Belloc has said, 'surely the only example in Europe of so modern an invention serving to protect the record of so remote a past'. After a short stretch of woodland we emerge on the bare slopes of Reigate Hill (756ft) and Colley Hill above a steep combe called the Horseshoe Down. Below is a hearthstone mine with a maze of passages in a specially hard variety of rock similar to that mined at Betchworth a mile or two further on; it is, of course, not open to the public. There are several National Trust holdings adding up to a sizeable area on the hill top. The route continues along Juniper Hill and Buckland Hills and through a wood to a B road just below the steep part of Pebblecombe Hill.

Ahead beyond the road are the huge scars of the Betchworth chalk pits. Lower down there used to be an extensive series of passages forming another hearthstone mine (once producing 200 tons a week). These were described by Harper and Kershaw in 1923, but access is no longer possible. The chalk pits are one of the outstanding landmarks of the Weald, conspicuous from as far away as the South Downs. The Pilgrims' Way traversed below the quarries, but the North Downs Way stays above the scarp along Betchworth Hill. It is wooded at first, but later there is open hillside, where it is possible, among other things, to sit and watch planes taking off from Gatwick. Spotters, armed with binoculars and radio sets, can comfortably do their logging from this distant grandstand. There is a parallel road by which the modern pilgrim can come to Box Hill, but the Way never needs to touch it. The flanks of Box Hill are open downland which can be traversed at will, the Pilgrims' Way stays at the lower end of the slope.

Box Hill is London's own mountain. Though only 563ft, it rises steeply from the Mole which here has cut a narrow gap

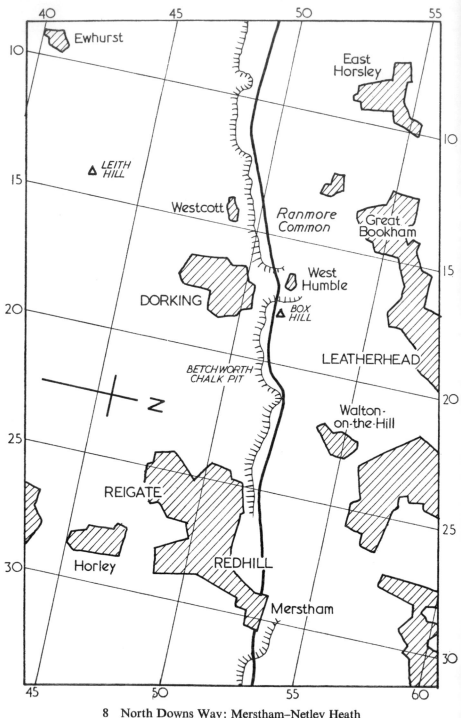

8 North Downs Way: Merstham–Netley Heath

through the chalk, thus giving the hill a memorable character. The name derives from the trees which clothe the western slopes, down which we descend by a remarkably steep route to stepping stones across the river. Alternatively one could go down the long open hillsides towards Burford Bridge, which are popular with skiers and tobogganers after winter snow-falls.

DORKING (TQ16/1748/49/50). At the crossing of A24 and A25, south of the Dorking gap where the Mole breaches the Downs. Main line railway station on a line between London and the coast, also on east-west line from Reading to Tonbridge. Youth Hostel at Tanner's Hatch (2½m). E.C. Wed.

Visit: Leith Hill (965ft)—summit tower tops 1,000ft (4½m SSW); Friday Street village (4m SW); Polesden Lacy, house and gardens (National Trust) (2½m NW); swallow holes northwards along the Mole valley; Box Hill (563ft) (1½m NE); Norbury Park (2m N).

The Way tunnels below A24 and the railway and climbs along the edge of a wood close to West Humble. Nearby is a man-made cave, now unfortunately in a dangerous condition, while on the Bookham road are the remains of a twelfth-century chapel having connections with the Pilgrims' Way. We continue over the shoulder marked 579ft to the road by Denbies and, passing the church, reach a road which has climbed the scarp from Dorking. At this point the line of the Pilgrims' Way is somewhat to the south. This is Ranmore Common (views and car parks) where there are big National Trust holdings, while a short distance northward are the Youth Hostel at Tanner's Hatch and the house and gardens of Polesden Lacy.

A few miles to the south are the Lower Greensand hills, which at Leith, Holmbury and Pitch Hills overtop us and cut off the view of the Weald. In between, and specially prominent in this section, lies the Vale of Holmesdale corresponding to the more easily eroded Upper Greensand and Gault clay. A combination of the chalk and sand ridges provides many a day walk for Londoners; the sand of course provides the view over the Weald which we usually associate with the chalk.

This section of down top is thickly wooded and the summits of the hills are difficult to locate. The route continues in and out of woods over White Down to the minor road from Effingham to Holmbury St Mary, which crosses here. There is a steep hill on the road and a spectacular viewpoint for motorists where it comes out of the trees on the scarp. We continue on the far side in more woods to Hackhurst Down (733ft), where there is a National Trust holding on the lower slopes, and on over Netley Heath eventually reaching Newlands Corner, where A25 crosses. One and a half miles north at West Clandon is Clandon Park (eighteenth century), while some way along the Leatherhead road beyond East Clandon is Hatchlands; both are National Trust. The terrain traversed by the Way hereabouts is complicated by woods, but there are plenty of paths. The Pilgrims' Way in this section was further south, probably passing through or near the villages of Gomshall and Shere and certainly south of the line of A25 up the scarp.

Newlands Corner nowadays is mostly a large car park; there are fine views across to the ridges of the Lower Greensand, and there are usually numbers of spectators to share them. After half a mile more on the scarp we descend it by a minor road to join the Pilgrims' Way lower down. We have left the chalk behind, the ridge continuing down into Guildford is of no interest to the walker.

GUILDFORD (around SU9949). Important road centre on A3 with numerous other access routes. Main line railway station—railway centre also. E.C. Wed.

The county town of Surrey, at the gap where the River Wey breached the chalk downs. Lively modern city with new cathedral, built during the last 40 years, and extensive University site. The keep of the Norman castle is preserved, with a small museum; extensive caves underneath are now closed to the public. *See*: Cathedral; St Mary's church (part Saxon); Guildhall (seventeenth century); sixteenth-century Grammar School with chained books; many old houses. *Visit*: Loseley House (Elizabethan) (2m S); Godalming Navigation (National Trust); Winkworth Arboretum (National Trust) (5m S); Shalford, old houses, water-mill and stocks (2m S); Great Tangley Manor (2½m SE); St Martha's Church, view (2m ESE); Albury Park, house and gardens (4½m ESE); Newlands Corner; Clandon Park (3m E); Hatchlands (4½m E); Sutton Place (3½m NE); the Hog's Back.

We join the Pilgrims' Way where it begins the ascent of St Martha's Hill, which is on the Lower Greensand. At the very top is St Martha's Church, rebuilt in the middle of the last century, which looks out over a wonderful view on all sides. We continue westwards across a minor road and descend the ridge called the Chantries to the River Wey Navigation, once crossed by ferry, where there will eventually be a bridge. After the railway we reach A3100; the continuation on the far side is a minor road a short distance to the right. This road is the line of the Pilgrims' Way, but soon the North Downs Way takes a parallel path immediately to the north. Nearby is Brabeouf Manor.

Above us half a mile to the north, the chalk ridge rises again at the start of the Hog's Back, which is continuous for 6 miles almost to Farnham. It carries the main road from Guildford (A31) and gives motorists wide views both north and south; scarp and dip sides of the ridge exhibit almost comparable steepness because the chalk strata here are tilted much more steeply than usual. 'One sees,' says Defoe, 'to the north over the great desert called Bagshot Heath one way, and the other way south-east into Sussex, almost to the South Downs, and west to an unbounded length . . .'

The Pilgrims' Way and the North Downs Way stay below the

southern scarp. At first the former is a minor road, the latter a path to its north, later they coincide as a minor road to a bridge below A3. Compton village (part-Norman church, picture gallery) is half a mile south. Beyond A3 Puttenham Heath is crossed, both routes coinciding, to Puttenham village. Hereabouts there is a cave, dug originally for glass sand; it used to be explorable, but is now no longer accessible. After a short stretch of road we cross Puttenham Common on a trackway passing south of Shoelands. To the south there is an earthwork and a considerable lake in Hampton Park; we carry on by a path which passes just south of Seale village, where the line of the Pilgrims' Way is identified as a minor road immediately to the north. We pass south of Sandy Cross and follow a complex of paths and trackways north of Crooksbury Hill to cross the River Wey by Moor Park College and reach the end of the North Downs Way. Crooksbury Hill only half a mile away is worth a diversion. It provides a splendid outlook across a typical piece of Surrey heath country towards the high hills by Hindhead.

FARNHAM (SU82 to 85E, 44 to 47N). On A31. Access by A325 from Aldershot, A287 from Hindhead, A325 from Petersfield and A287 from Odiham. Main line railway station. E.C. Wed.
    See: old houses and inns; Farnham Grange in Castle Hill (National Trust); castle, ruins of shell keep. *Visit*: Crooksbury Hill (2½m E); Frensham Ponds (3m S).

Now we have lost touch with the chalk and there is no really satisfactory line on westwards. Both the Pilgrims' Way and the Harrow Way followed the lines of present day roads in their onward journeys. The Pilgrims' Way crossed the watershed somewhere beyond Alton and so came to Winchester, while the Harrow Way aimed for Ellisfield Camp (SU6245) south of Basingstoke.
    After passing above Alton travellers aiming to link with the

South Downs Way make for Selborne. The west-bound traveller on the other hand, turning north-west at first towards Ellisfield Camp, will find nothing but minor roads all the way to Andover. The best walkers' route to the west is undoubtedly the Inkpen Ridgeway which can be joined at Cottington's Hill.

There is little joy in the Harrow Way, as the line is entirely obliterated by the complex road system at Andover. Just before entering the Salisbury Plain area at Cholderton on the River Bourne there is the outstanding camp of Quarley Hill (557ft), about one and a half miles south of A303 between there and Grateley. Hippisley Cox says of it: 'Close at hand it is difficult to realise that its gentle slopes should stand out so distinctly when seen from distant uplands, where Quarley often proves useful in giving the direction of trackways, and is as welcome to the view as Fuji to the Japanese.'

References
O.S. 1 inch Map Sheets 169, 170
O.S. 2½ inch Map Sheets SU84, 94, TU04, 14, 15, 25

THE INKPEN RIDGEWAY

Basingstoke–Cottington's Hill–Kingsclere–Ladle Hill
Beacon Hill (Newbury)–Pilot Hill–Walbury Hill–Inkpen Hill
(Hungerford)–Fosbury Camp–Chute Causeway
Collingbourne Kingston

The west-bound traveller on the Harrow Way arriving in the neighbourhood of Basingstoke and making for places north of Stonehenge has an alternative open to him along another fine scarp edge, which falls to the valley of the Kennet. Hippisley Cox sites the parting of the ways at the tiny Ellisfield Camp (SU6245) but there are no footpaths in the countryside to encourage starting here nowadays. The Ridgeway leads to the northern edge of

E

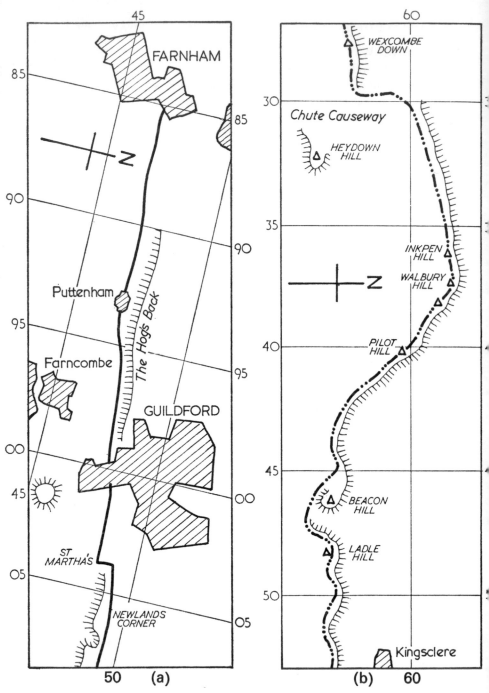

9 (a) North Downs Way: Netley Heath–Farnham; (b) Inkpen Ridgeway

Salisbury Plain above the Vale of Pewsey or, by crossing the watershed between the Kennet and the Avon, the traveller could come to the Wansdyke Ridgeway. The name 'Inkpen Ridgeway' is that used by Timperley and Brill.

Here are the highest hills in the English chalk country, though those to the north of the Vale of Pewsey run them close. Inkpen Hill (Beacon), long credited with 1,011ft, was later demoted, and precise measurements settled on Walbury Hill (974ft) as the highest. It is not specially impressive with cultivation carried right across an extensive flat summit of considerable area (100 acres above the 900ft contour).

Basingstoke to Cottington's Hill is 8½ miles; it is 10 miles further to Pilot Hill, then another 2 to Walbury Hill. Walbury Hill to Collingbourne Kingston and the Bourne crossing is 10½ miles making a total of 31 miles.

Winklebury Camp is surrounded nowadays by the houses of Basingstoke. The land slopes up gradually to the beginnings of the ridge; just beyond Hannington we cross the line of the Roman Portway (Silchester to Old Sarum) and immediately beyond find Cottington's Hill (753ft). This is crossed to White Hill where B3051 from Kingsclere to Overton climbs steeply up the scarp. After Watership Hill (778ft), said to look like an inverted boat, and a minor road crossing, pathways lead to Ladle Hill (767ft) where there is an extremely interesting hill fort. The construction was never completed, so that examination and excavation of the terrain have taught archaeologists a great deal about the actual construction methods which were used. At this point A34 runs through a low pass in the hill line which would have been particularly strongly defended by this camp in conjunction with that on Beacon Hill on the far side. The route follows the scarp southwesterly down to this road by Seven Barrows, crosses and climbs the spur of Woodcott Down ahead. Beacon Hill, one and a half miles north, is not readily accessible from here; however, below it on the road is a large car park. The ramparts half a mile in circumference are built round the 800ft contour and entirely enclose the summit. Six miles to the north is:

NEWBURY (SU46 to 48E, 65 to 68N). Access by A4 from east and west, by A34 from Winchester and Oxford, by A343 from Andover. Main line railway station. E.C. Wed.

At the junction of the Rivers Kennet and Lambourn, the adjacent section of the Kennet–Avon Canal is still operational and this length is being extended. Two battles were fought here in the Civil War, in 1643 to the south-west by the Andover road and in 1644 outside Donnington Castle to the north. *See*: church (sixteenth century); Cloth Hall, now a museum; Racecourse; Donnington Castle (gatehouse only); the Falkland Memorial (National Trust), which commemorates the Royalists killed in the First Battle of Newbury. *Visit*: Woolton Hall, nature reserve (National Trust) (3m SW).

The Ridgeway continues to Sidown Hill (872ft), where there are woods on the northern flanks, and on down to A343 close to Ashmansworth. The way runs on north-westerly and in 2½ miles we reach Pilot Hill (937ft), which surprisingly is the county summit of Hampshire. A few hundred yards on bring us into Berkshire. In this section the scarp slopes are particularly steep and impressive, while in places the valleys on the dip side have cut back so far that there are extensive two-way views. We leave the summit of Combe Hill (953ft) on our left on a spur, close to which there is road access from north and south. Straight ahead leads up to Walbury Hill (974ft), highest chalk hill in England, county summit of Berkshire and highest hill within 80 miles of London. The summit camp is a single bank, a mile in circumference. The actual highest point is off to the south side of the track in the middle of a large field. When I was last there it was occupied by a military or industrial communications vehicle actively communicating. Hippisley Cox draws attention to the great suitability of the site for a beacon: '... as Winchester, which could be approached from the sea, is only twenty miles to the south with sloping ground all the way, whilst to the north beyond the Kennet, a ridgeway follows rising ground to White Horse Hill, also only twenty miles distant. From White Horse Hill, just short of one thousand feet high, the whole of the valley of the Upper Thames is within view, with Dunstable on the east and Malvern on the west, neither too far off to receive and send warning lights.'

Another road access point, with car parks, is followed by Combe Gibbet, a grisly reminder of a more barbarous past, which has to be maintained, it is said, under the terms of the lease of a nearby farm. A scarecrow hanging from the cross-arm presents a daunting sight at all times, but even more so when it is dark, cold, or for some other reason deserted. The next hill, Inkpen Hill, has an interesting history for, probably in confusion with its neighbours, it had the reputation of being over 1,000ft high, which would take away all the above credits from Walbury Hill, as well as providing south-east England with what might well be called a mountain. But the measurers were proved to be wrong and it is only 954ft. It is said that, when the pre-eminence of Walbury Hill was realised, Berkshire shifted its boundaries with Hampshire so as to retain the highest summit of the range. Berkshire certainly has it today. A southern spur of Inkpen Hill is called Sheepless Hill, drawing attention perhaps to its unsuitability in past times for even the staple usage of downland.

The scarp continues to be steep. The trackway descends gradually over Ham Hill (841ft), Rivar Hill and Rivar Down. Between here and Botley Hill a mysterious ditch of unknown purpose parallels the way for three quarters of a mile. There are a number of minor road crossings. Four and a half miles to the north is:

HUNGERFORD (SU3367/68). Access by A4 from east and west, by A419 from Swindon, by A338 from Salisbury and Wantage. Main line railway station. E.C. Thurs.

Where the Kennet–Avon Canal diverges from the Kennet valley to climb over the watershed to the Vale of Pewsey.

See: the Hocktide ceremony on the Tuesday of Easter week; Bear Inn. *Visit*: Littlecote House (sixteenth century) (2½m NW); Inkpen and Walbury Hills (5m SE); Avington, Norman church (2m E).

The hill line turns southwards and we follow it by trackway and minor road to Tidcombe Down and Tidcombe Long Barrow.

At this point a south-westerly spur of hill rising to Point 860 and to Haydown Hill (845ft) is particularly striking. On the latter is Fosbury Camp, three quarters of a mile in circumference with double lines of high banks and a deep ditch between. The Roman road from Winchester towards Marlborough has to make a considerable semi-circular detour here, as though the road-makers, using the hill as a marker for their alignment, went ahead until confronted with the steep descent into Hippenscombe. This forced them up a ridge, almost certainly on the line of an earlier trackway, and around the head of the combe until they could regain their direction on the other side. The detour is known as Chute Causeway.

The continuing line of the Roman road indicates probably the most satisfactory connection between this ridgeway and the Wansdyke Ridgeway on the hills north of the Vale of Pewsey. The Kennet–Avon Canal has to be crossed either at the summit tunnel between Stibb Green and Durley or further east at Crofton (where the original pumping engine for the upper reaches of the Canal is being carefully preserved and should not be missed in passing). Indeed this crossing of the watershed between the Kennet and the Avon probably gave a well-drained, marsh-free route in early times.

The last hill on the main ridge is Wexcombe Down (874ft), below is Collingbourne Kingston on the Bourne and Salisbury Plain.

References
O.S. 1 inch Map Sheets 167, 168
O.S. 2½ inch Map Sheets SU55, 45, 36, 26, 25

4

THE SOUTH DOWNS WAY

Eastbourne–Jevington (or *Beachy Head–Cuckmere*)–*Alfriston*
Firle Beacon–Southease (or *Glynde–Cliffe Hill*
Lewes–Mount Harry)–*Black Cap*

WHEREAS the chalk ridgeways of our ancestors, and the modern ramblers' routes which substantially follow them, usually take a line above the steepest part of the scarp, this first section of the South Downs Way presents an alternative—some five miles of cliff edge over Beachy Head and the Seven Sisters, which contrasts sharply with the typical downland line. Further on beyond Firle Beacon the official route crosses the Ouse at Southease and climbs on to the Downs again beyond Lewes, but it is also possible to descend to the Glynde River, cross Cliffe Hill, traverse Lewes and then follow the Downs again over Mount Harry.

By the path, Eastbourne to Jevington is 3¾ miles and Jevington to Alfriston is a further 3¾; it is 4½ miles to the West Firle road access point, whence a further 3½ miles lead to Southease village. From here to the A27 crossing is 6 miles and then 3 miles more to Black Cap. The shortest distance therefore is 24½ miles. The detour by the cliffs (7 miles from Eastbourne to Exceat and 3 miles from Exceat to Alfriston) adds 2½ miles to the overall trip. The detour by Lewes on the other hand (West Firle road access point to Lewes 5 miles, 1 mile through urban Lewes and 2½ miles on to Black Cap), not actually part of the Way, is 4 miles shorter than the official route.

At one time the chalk ridges of southern England were continuous with those of France beyond the Channel. Then some 7,000 years ago the sea broke through slicing across the South Downs to leave some impressive sea-cliffs. Eastbourne has grown up in the shelter of this chalk wall.

EASTBOURNE (around TV6199). Access by A22 from London or A259 along the coast. Main line terminus. E.C. Thurs.

See: Pier and parades; Wish Tower (Martello Tower); Holywell Art Gallery. *Visit*: Beachy Head (2½m SW) and Birling Gap (4m WSW); Pevensey Castle (4m NE).

The main route of the South Downs Way starts at O.S. ref 598983 from which there is a track leading to the Brighton–Eastbourne road (A259) and on northwards along the edge of the scarp above the Old Town to Willingdon Hill (659ft). Now we can look back eastwards over Pevensey Levels, which with gently sloping beach and flat hinterland have long encouraged the illicit landing of armies notably that of William the Norman and of cargoes. The defences of various ages still remain in the Roman Anderida, the Norman keep within the same walls and the Martello Towers which line the shores.

The hill ridge runs north to Combe Hill, where there are remains of a Neolithic causewayed enclosure, but the Way descends westwards down Bourne Hill to Jevington village (ancient Saxon church tower). We cross B2105 and climb out again on the far side, north-westwards, to Windover Hill on the scarp edge above Wilmington. The highest point hereabouts, somewhat to the right of the route, is Wilmington Hill (702ft), steeply scarped, with the long barrow of Hunters' Burgh on a north-easterly spur. There is a long barrow, too, on Windover Hill above the huge carved figure of the Long Man of Wilmington, 230ft long, which probably dates from the Middle Ages, when it marked from afar the site of Wilmington Priory below. There are other versions of his origin; the staves clasped in either hand were shown as a scythe and a rake in MS of the eighteenth century. The present outline was delineated in white brick in 1873, previously it had been necessary to scour periodically as with other hill figures. The Way now descends the slopes of the Cuckmere Valley to Alfriston.

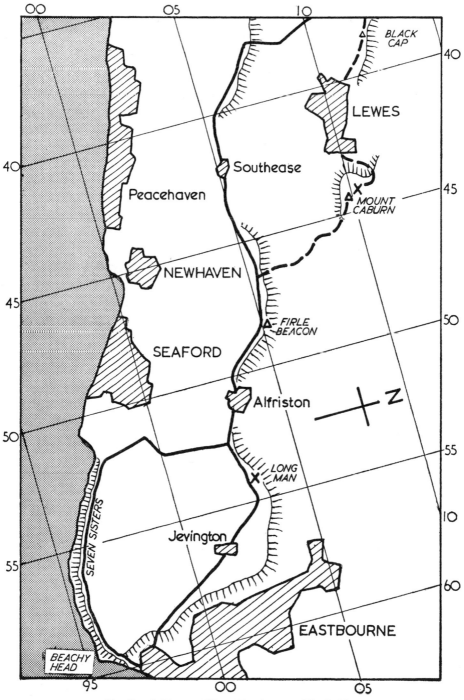

10   South Downs Way: Eastbourne–Black Cap

The alternative line starts at the west end of Eastbourne promenade where the hills tilt up sharply above Holywell and one soon surmounts the old scarp face. The top of Beachy Head, only just over a mile ahead, no longer disfigured by radar installations, is fine indeed. The cliffs are high (534ft) and vertical, giving an almost mountain experience; as Frank Smythe, the well-known mountaineer, has said of them: 'Anyone who can gaze unmoved upon the sea from the edge of Beachy Head need have no qualms as to his reactions upon the most sensational of Alpine precipices.' Before the turn of the century this was a famous rock-climbing area, but so soft is the rock that the pinnacles which used to adorn the face—the seven Charles's—are all but one fallen into the sea. During the 1950s the redoubtable Devil's Chimney, which had a literature of its own, subsided to the sea and was washed away, leaving only the quaintly named Etheldreda's Pinnacle to link with the glories of the past. Owing to the exigencies of the cross-channel shipping lanes the packet from Dieppe, Newhaven bound, aims for Beachy Head and then turns and sweeps westward along the coast. The spectacle should be magnificent, but, sad to say, the cliffs look less impressive then, somewhat dirty and streaked with brown stains.

Soon the cliffs are steeper still; above the lighthouse and on towards Belle Tout they are at least vertical if not actually overhanging, and the edge should be approached with care. The modern lighthouse was built at sea level in 1901, replacing the earlier structure on the cliff top, on the usual principle that the higher a light the more often is it obscured by mist. In this case too the Head itself cut off the view of the old light in the easterly sector. The buildings at Belle Tout, dating to 1831, were partly demolished by pointless target practice during the last war. The path runs down to Birling Gap, where there is a hotel, coastguard cottages and a car park (road access from West Dean). The cliffs are being eroded steadily—the Way has already had to be diverted once. The staircase to the stony beach often requires repairs after a rough winter.

One other possible route for the adventurous traveller from

Eastbourne should be noted—a traverse of the beach. It should only be attempted by the confident on a falling tide, and the state of the exit at Birling Gap must be known in advance, but it is well worth the effort as the cliffs certainly impress when seen from below.

Now come the Seven Sisters, vertically truncated ends of a series of ridges between dry valleys in the chalk; half of them are National Trust. After two undulating miles over the only unspoilt cliff line in the south-east of England we reach the flat bottomed gap cut by the Cuckmere River, some half a mile wide; the Way follows the east bank inland to Exceat Bridge, through the recently created Seven Sisters Country Park. Here, where A259 crosses the river, the route doubles back to the east for a quarter of a mile, and finally makes for Westdean village, where Alfred the Great is said to have held court in 884. There is a bust by Epstein in the church. We continue past Charleston Manor to Litlington (ancient church), with a view on the way over to the White Horse on Hindover Hill, and so down to Alfriston. A short distance north of the route is the minute church of Lullington, claimed to be the smallest in England. Since it is only 16ft square this is probably so, though it is in fact the remains of a larger structure. Off to the east is Lullington Nature Reserve.

ALFRISTON (TQ5103). On B2108. Nearest station—Berwick (main line) 2¼ miles. Youth Hostel. E.C. Wed.

See: Church ('the Cathedral of the South Downs'); Old Clergy House; Market Cross; *Star* and *George* inns. *Visit*: Lullington Church (¾m E); the Long Man of Wilmington and Wilmington Priory ruin (2m E); traces of a White Horse at Hindover Hill.

Leaving the village the Way climbs north-westwards, past Long Burgh, a 180ft long barrow. The church at Berwick below the scarp shows some startling modern decoration. We continue over Bostal Hill (624ft) to Firle Beacon (713ft); the scarp slopes are steep and the view over the Weald is extensive. Hereabouts we come across a large crop of prehistoric remains including round and bell barrows. Beyond Firle, road access from West Firle offers alternative routes for the next section.

The Way continues ahead over Beddingham Hill (623ft, radio masts) and down the long shoulder of Iford Hill into the wide valley of the Ouse, here only a few miles from its mouth at Newhaven. To the north, beyond the water meadows, is the substantial town of Lewes. We cross the railway at Southease and Rodmell station, then the river, reaching A275 on the far side. The nearby villages of Rodmell, Kingston and Piddinghoe all have interesting churches. After Rodmell village the Way climbs steadily north-westwards along the scarp edge over Front Hill and Iford Hill, until we arrive above Kingston, then turns west to Castle Hill. Ahead is Newmarket Hill, which looks down on Woodingdean and Brighton, but our route swinging north descends a spur to A27 at Newmarket Inn, crossing the Lewes–Brighton railway en route. On the far side a track on Balmer Down leads back to the main line of the Downs near Black Cap (677ft) on top of the steep north-facing scarp.

Descending into the valley from the neighbourhood of Firle, the alternative route passes Glynde station and then climbs on to Cliffe Hill (538ft), formerly part of the Down line, now isolated by gaps cut by the Glynde and Ouse rivers. There is a fine hill fort on the southerly spur called Mount Caburn and huge quarries face down to Lewes. To the west the steep slopes of Malling Hill were the scene of a fatal snow avalanche during the severe winter of 1837. 'One of the streets of Lewes runs by the side of immense rocks or hills, and upon the setting of a very sudden thaw, down came an enormous mass of snow. Cottages were overwhelmed, several persons perished . . .' Down below, and quickly reached, is:

LEWES (TQ40/4109/10). Access by A27 from Brighton and

Eastbourne, A275 from East Grinstead and Newhaven, A26 from Tunbridge Wells. Main line station. E.C. Wed.

The county town of Sussex, this has been an important site since days long ago when the Ouse was a wide estuary and this was the location of the first bridge. There were some fortifications here before the present castle was built. *See*: Castle (which, unusually, had two mottes); Barbican House Museum; Anne of Cleves's house; St Anne's Church (twelfth century).

The battle of Lewes was fought on the slopes of Mount Harry to the west. The contestants were King Henry III and Simon de Montfort, the victory gained by the latter led on to the founding of the first parliament in this country. There is a commemorating stone. The track passes the battlefield, then the former racecourse, crosses Mount Harry (639ft) and so comes to Black Cap, where the main line of the Way is rejoined.

References
O.S. 1 inch Map Sheet 183
O.S. 2½ inch Map Sheets TV59, TQ50, 40, 30, 31

BLACK CAP TO CHANCTONBURY HILL

Black Cap–Ditchling Beacon (Brighton)–Devil's Dyke
Bramber–Steyning–Chanctonbury Hill (Worthing)

Over the first part the coastline gradually converges on the line of the Downs, until at the crossing of the River Adur they are only 3 miles apart. Thereafter the coastline bulges and the two diverge. Unfortunately the near proximity of the sea adds little to the charm of the hills. The seaward slopes are much built over —the coast itself being left almost entirely without any features of natural beauty. Civilisation spreads up the dip slope towards the scarp edge in the form of power lines, golf courses, radar stations, housing estates and so on, while the resorts send up their pilgrims, notably to the Devil's Dyke, once the terminus of a light railway from Brighton, now fed similarly by a motor road.

Here the Downs are at their most majestic; their smooth flowing outlines epitomise exactly our ideas of what hills, as distinct from mountains, really should be; the comparative lack of trees gives continuous far-ranging views over the toy-like landscape of the Weald to the far-off gleam of the chalk pits of the North Downs beyond. Yet it is one particular tree clump, that specially planted more than two centuries ago near the summit of Chanctonbury Hill, which dominates the view of these hills from a distance—far and away their most recognisable landmark. As sea and down diverge, the ridges and valleys of the dip slope are often found to be interesting and worthy of attention.

The walking distances are as follows: Black Cap to Ditchling Beacon road access $2\frac{1}{2}$ miles, on to the Brighton road (A23) 3 miles and on again to Devil's Dyke a further $2\frac{1}{2}$ miles. It is 2 miles from Devil's Dyke to Truleigh Hill road access, whence the eventual route via Botolphs will lead in $5\frac{1}{2}$ miles to Steyning Round Hill. The diversions through Bramber and Steyning may be slightly further. Another 2 miles lead to Chanctonbury Hill— a total of $17\frac{1}{2}$ miles.

The traveller on the Way who has come over Balmer Down from Newmarket Inn reaches the scarp edge a short distance west of Black Cap (677ft). The ridge rises gently over Plumpton Plain where there are two small earthworks. Below on the scarp a V-shaped plantation celebrates Queen Victoria's Diamond Jubilee. In $2\frac{1}{2}$ miles from Black Cap we reach the highest point of this bare western section of the Sussex Downs—Ditchling Beacon (813ft). There is a summit earthwork 300yd in diameter. A minor road which has climbed steeply up the scarp from Ditchling village, crossing at this point on its way to Brighton, gives road access. Four and a half acres of the north-eastern slopes are National Trust property. Along the ridge east and west of

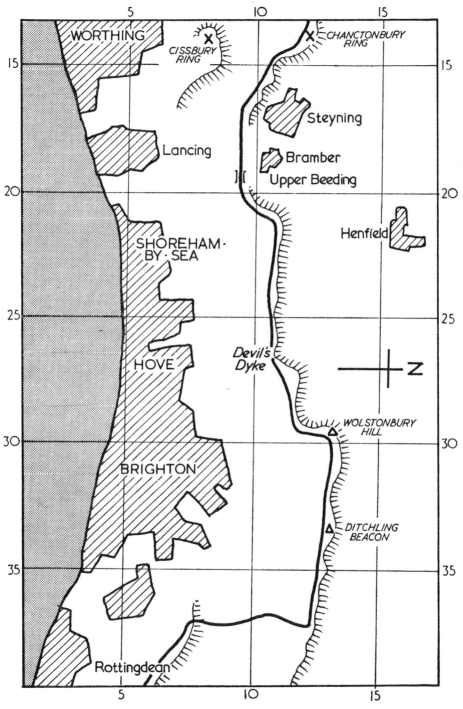

11 South Downs Way: Black Cap–Chanctonbury Hill

Ditchling, Hippisley Cox counted more than 100 tumuli, we pass many of them, and also some dew ponds, on our way to Point 765, 1 mile ahead. On the south-east spur of this hill above Patcham is the Chattri, a memorial to the Indian troops who died in the 1914–18 War, actually erected on the site of the ghat where bodies were cremated. Here we are on the outskirts of:

BRIGHTON and HOVE (around TQ30/3104/05). Access by A27 from Lewes and from Worthing and by A23 from London. Main line railway terminus. Youth Hostel at Patcham (3 miles). E.C. Wed, or Thurs, or Sat.

A highly developed resort offering every sort of facility. Until 1783 it was the tiny village of Brighthelmstone; then the Prince Regent, afterwards King George IV, began the visits which led to its development as a resort. *See*: Sea front; Piers; the Aquarium; Royal Pavilion; Museum and Art Gallery; Booth Museum of British Birds; Black Rock Railway; Hollingbury Castle (earthworks); the 'Lanes'; West Blatchington Windmill. *Visit*: Devil's Dyke (5m NW).

The Way continues westwards almost to Clayton windmills— Jack, the black one, Jill the other—then doubles back left to avoid their approach road. Soon a trackway leads west again dropping down to A273, at a point 1 mile south of Clayton village. This is notable for three things—the unique pair of windmills already passed, the Saxon church with Norman wall-paintings and the unusual architecture of the northern mouth of Clayton Tunnel which, built in the 1840s, looks like a castle gate-house.

The tunnel is beneath our feet as we follow a short stretch of minor road through to A23, from which the Way climbs thankfully straight ahead up a spur of Newtimber Hill. To the north jutting out ahead of the down line is one of the outstanding hills of the South Downs—Wolstonbury Hill (677ft)—'the noblest in mien of the whole range by virtue of its isolation and its conical

(*left*) Ditchling Beacon, looking east along the Downs

Page 86 (*above*) Box Hill; (*below*) Combe Gibbet, with Walbury Hill
beyond

shape'. The sides are scarred with quarries, but the top carries a fine circular camp with pit dwellings, while there is an excellent view along the scarps on either hand.

The top of Newtimber Hill, a substantial National Trust holding, is long and flat with the highest point (664ft) at the northern end above the scarp. The Way crosses the summit further south and descends towards Saddlescombe, to which there is access by minor road from Poynings.

Ahead now is the Devil's Dyke, a steep-sided dry valley, dug originally by the Devil to let the sea into the Weald. Due to accident-proneness, surprising in one of such exceptional powers, he usually failed when engaged on projects of this sort, and this was no exception. Nevertheless we have to commend the results of his labours. The far side of the Dyke is a promontory (711ft) ringed by an ancient encampment, which carries also the shrines of the modern pilgrims. This point is particularly accessible to Brighton, even though the trains are no more, and the very fine view must be taken in company.

The scarp continues to be very steep and the Way takes it, as on top of a wall, over Fulking Hill (658ft) and Perching Hill (over 550ft). At the next gap two power lines come striding up from Southwick, cross and divide into three at the northern foot. Edburton Hill (583ft) beyond carries an earthwork which has been identified (surprisingly) as a one-time motte and bailey castle. It is difficult to appreciate the utility of this site in terms of Norman control of conquered Saxons and it may well date from the later troubled times of King Stephen, when a great deal of temporary castle building took place. On Truleigh Hill (708ft), three-quarters of a mile further west, there used to be a radar station; we reach the approach road close to the Youth Hostel at Tottington Barn. From this point a prominent ridge leads east of south over Thundersbarrow Hill (491ft, remains of ancient village and field system) to Southwick Hill, a National Trust property looking down on Southwick and the sea.

A possible diversion here is to descend to Upper Beeding and follow main roads for a mile to Bramber, or follow a footpath

F

(not suitable as a bridleway) further north through Upper Beeding, cross the river by a footbridge at Kings Barn and so come to Steyning.

STEYNING (TQ1710/11), BRAMBER (TQ1810/11) and UPPER BEEDING (TQ1910). Access by A283 from Shoreham and the west and by A2037 from the north. Nearest station—Shoreham (4m). Youth Hostel at Tottington Barn (Truleigh Hill). E.C. Thurs.

A contiguous series of towns/villages. Charles II came near to capture at Bramber before finally escaping from Shoreham. At Steyning—*See*: Norman church; Market Hall. At Bramber —*See*: Castle ruins (with motte formed by digging across a spur, and view to Leith Hill); Potter Museum; St Mary's House (fifteenth century). *Visit*: Botolphs (site of ancient seaport before the haven silted up at Shoreham) (1m S); Coombes (ancient church) (1½m S).

The Way will pass to the south of these places, plunging down a spur of Beeding Hill to cross the Adur by a new bridge north of Lock Barn, here only 3 miles from its mouth. A short stretch of minor road through Botolphs will lead on to the ridge of Annington Hill and up to the minor road from Steyning to Sompting. Three quarters of a mile south is Steep Down (489ft) from which Beachy Head, the Isle of Wight, Devil's Dyke and Black Down (Haslemere) can all be seen on a clear day. There is said to be a startling effect at sunset when the sun is reflected in the windows of Brighton, 'so that town and piers appear a blaze of fire'. The church at Sompting is well worth a visit; it dates from the tenth century and has a most unusual gabled spire. Further west is the urban sprawl of Worthing.

The Way will follow this minor road northwards for half a mile, being joined on the way by the alternative route through Bramber, which climbs the combe between Annington Hill and Steyning Round Hill. When our road turns on to a shoulder of the latter, we continue by trackway to the summit at 619ft. Travellers who have come by the more northerly route through Steyning rejoin here.

Now at last woodlands begin to appear on the scarp of the hills, a feature which becomes more prominent as we move further westwards. As yet the views are unimpeded. Passing the magnificent Elizabethan manor of Wiston in the valley below the scarp and the archaeological site of Park Brow a mile down the dip, the edge climbs steadily to Chanctonbury Hill (782ft). Five hundred yards short of the summit is Chanctonbury Ring, a small earthwork of 3 acres, which became the outstanding landmark of the Downs when a clump of beech trees was planted here in 1760. Even on a bright day it is somehow eerie in the wood as though it enclosed something of the prehistoric aura of the site. Roman remains have also been discovered hereabouts.

Two and a half miles to the south is Cissbury Ring, the biggest earthwork in Sussex. Surrounding the summit (602ft) of a hill looking down on Worthing, it has an area of upwards of 60 acres, with a circumference of more than a mile. It dates to the Iron Age (300 BC), but was later used by the Romans and then by the Britons against the Saxons. It is said that 35,000 cubic yd of chalk were excavated to build the ramparts and that 10,000 timber baulks of 15ft were used in the retaining walls. Why was it so large? 'The easy communication with the sea,' says Hippisley Cox, 'suggests its use as a depot for commerce and shipping.' There were extensive flint mines both inside and outside the ring. Close below is:

WORTHING (around TQ1403). Access by A27 from Brighton and from Chichester, A2032 from Littlehampton, A24 from London. Main line railway station. E.C. Wed.

A seaside resort with a longer history than might be imagined. Erosion has altered the coastline considerably, but it seems probable that a haven hereabouts would account for the location and size of Cissbury Camp. There was certainly a village, or town, here in the reign of Edward III. Grew as a resort in the same period as Brighton. *See*: Museum and Art Gallery. *Visit*: Sompting church (2m NE); Cissbury Ring (3½m N); High Salvington windmill (2½m N); Blackpatch and Harrow Hills (5m NW); Highdown Hill (earthworks and Saxon burial ground) (3½m WNW).

References
O.S. 1 inch Map Sheets 182, 183
O.S. 2½ inch Map Sheets TQ31, 21, 20, 10, 11

CHANCTONBURY HILL TO COCKING

Chanctonbury Hill–Amberley Station (Amberley, Pulborough, Arundel, Littlehampton)–Stane Street–Duncton Down (Petworth)–Graffham Down–Cocking (Midhurst)–the Trundle (Chichester)

In this section is the highest point of the Sussex South Downs (836ft) variously called Tegleaze, Littleton Down or Duncton Down—an undistinguished summit in the heart of a wood. (Undistinguished because it is neither the highest point in Sussex, which is Black Down [919ft], nor the highest of the South Downs, which is Butser Hill [888ft] in Hampshire.) After the Arun Gap the hill slopes become more densely wooded than heretofore. As the scarp edge diverges further from the coast, there is room at first for a system of hill ridges and valleys running from north to south in the dip slope. Then the coastal plain widens too as we reach the meadows of Chichester and the flats of Selsey.

On the north side of the Weald the North Downs are paralleled for a greater part of their length by a ridge of Lower Greensand which sometimes overtops the chalk. In the south this sandstone ridge, while never so prominent, begins to obtrude west of the Arun. The western Rother runs parallel to the Downs in the valley between the formations to join the Arun at Pulborough. The sand is over 400ft on either side of Petworth, reaches 625ft at Bexley Hill, north-east of Midhurst and 676ft at Telegraph Hill a few miles further on. To the north the Greensand is even higher at Black Down by Haslemere. These various hills set a limit to the northerly view.

By the Way it is 1 mile from Chanctonbury Hill to the crossing of the Washington By-pass and then $6\frac{1}{2}$ miles to Amberley Station. From here to the Stane Street crossing is 6 miles, a further 2 miles lead to the gap by Duncton where A285 crosses, whence it is $5\frac{1}{2}$ miles to A286 crossing by Cocking. The total for this section is therefore 21 miles.

From Chanctonbury Hill a straightforward mile leads to A24 immediately south of Washington. The Way crosses the Washington By-pass on the level, but bridle-way users can avoid this by a detour to the north, crossing on a bridge leading out of Washington village and rejoining the route on Barnsfarm Hill. Worthing is 5 miles south of this point.

The Way now climbs from A24 up Highden Hill to Barnsfarm Hill (675ft) and on over Sullington Hill, where there is an ancient embankment above the scarp, to Chantry Hill. There is road access to this point from Storrington. Two southerly spurs end in the important archaeological sites of Blackpatch Hill (555ft) (flint mine sites and round barrows) and Harrow Hill (549ft) (flint mine sites and an Iron Age fort). Ancient track ways led on southwards to Highdown Hill (National Trust) above Ferring, where there is an earthwork and where an extensive Saxon burial ground was excavated in 1893.

On Kithurst Hill the Way reaches 700ft. At the next col (1 mile), after passing what the O.S. Map calls a 'Danger Area' on the scarp face, there is access by a steep minor road. This leads down to B2139 at the hill foot, beyond which is Parham House, an Elizabethan manor, open to the public during the summer months. Over Rackham Hill, past Rackham Banks earthworks and over Amberley Mount we come down to the road south of Amberley village.

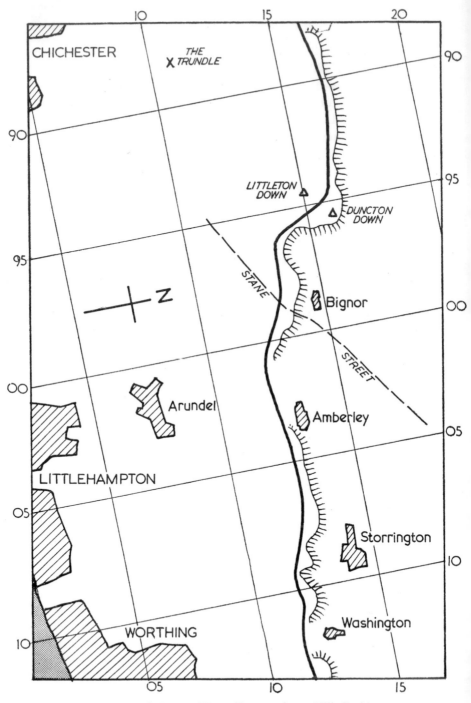

12 South Downs Way: Chanctonbury Hill–Cocking

AMBERLEY (TQ02/0313). Access by minor roads off B2139. Main line railway station (1m). E.C. Wed.

The very picturesque castle is inhabited and not open to the public (except for occasional admission to the gardens only). *See*: thirteenth-century church.

Amberley Station is reached on B2139 which runs below a large quarry on the Downs east of the gap. We cross the railway and the river and follow the road to Houghton, turn right into a minor road for a quarter of a mile, then left again by a track up a spur of Bury Hill to A284. Five miles north of here is:

PULBOROUGH (TQ0518). Access by A29 from north and south, A283 from east and west. Main line railway station. E.C. Wed.

This is where Stane Street crossed the Arun, the exact manner of the crossing is still unresolved. Hardham Camp to the south was a staging point on the road which runs uncompromisingly straight from here to Dorking Gap.

South of the gap at Amberley the traveller with time on his hands may diverge to:

ARUNDEL (TQ00/0106/07). Access by A284 from north and south and by A27 from east and west. Main line railway station. Youth Hostel at Warningcamp (1m). E.C. Wed.

The guidebook calls Arundel 'unquestionably one of the most idyllic spots in England . . . a huge castle, the foundations of which were laid centuries ago but whose walls look fresh and fair, a church cathedral-like in proportions . . .' Some parts of the castle are Norman; the circular keep 60ft in diameter stands on a 70ft motte. It was extensively restored during the last century and is still inhabited (regularly opened to the public). *See*: Castle; parish church; Fitzalan Chapel; The

Park (with tower, lake and earthworks). *Visit*: Burpham (with earthwork which defends the passage of the river) (1½m NE); churches at Climping, Yapton, Ford and Tortington (all within 3m SW); the modern resort of Littlehampton (3½m SSE).

The Way now climbs over Bury Hill and Westburton Hill to Bignor Hill (737ft). This is in the National Trust holding of Slindon Estate which includes also Slindon Park to the south, Coldharbour Hill and most of the Neolithic causewayed camp of Barkhale beside the Way. To the south-east between here and Arundel Park in the woods south of Fairmile Bottom lies, says Massingham, 'a network of earthworks, ditches and covered and terraced ways some three miles in length. They are so labyrinthine that I for one got hopelessly lost among them. But the Celtic city of Rewell Hill, far larger than anything Roman in England, of which this maze is only the archives, is more utterly lost in time than I ever was in direction.'

Back on the Way we soon reach the col (684ft) where the Roman Stane Street crossed the crest of the Downs. There is road access by a steep lane from Bignor. From this point the Roman road plunged down the scarp and then made a bee-line for Hardham Camp and the river crossing at Pulborough, passing close to the fine Roman villa at Bignor uncovered in 1811. This is outstanding and should on no account be missed. The original residence covered 5 acres and had some fifty rooms. Some very fine mosaic pavements have been left open for inspection and there is a museum. On the dip slope Stane Street takes a straight line to Chichester which was the Roman Noviomagus. It follows trackways at first but near Halnaker Hill, with its fort and windmill, the line is taken over by the modern A285.

There now follows an appreciable diversion from the scarp edge, which here turns northwards from Coldharbour Hill (803ft) over Farm Hill to Barlavington Down. The early ridgeway probably went this way, turning west again over the col at Duncton Down, now crossed by A285, and then climbing straight ahead up Woolavington Down. The South Downs Way, however, skirts Coldharbour Hill on the south to Burton Down and descends a north-westerly spur to Littleton Farm on A285, 1½ miles south of where it crosses the scarp. Beyond the road our route forges ahead on to Woolavington Down, which is in fact a shoulder of Point 836 (Teglease, Littleton Down, Duncton Down—the name is obscure) the summit of the Sussex Downs. The traveller who seeks to tread this point will have to take to the woods hereabouts; there seems little point in so doing. Four and a half miles west of north and worth a visit is:

PETWORTH (SU9721). Access by A272 from the east and west, A283 from the north, A280 and A283 from the south. Nearest station Pulborough (5½m). E.C. Wed.

A pleasant country town with old streets and houses. *See*: Petworth House (National Trust) and park.

From Woolavington Down the Way continues, with woods now on both dip and scarp, over Graffham Down and Point 763 to Heyshott Down (766ft), passing some round barrows en route. The slopes of Manorfarm Down lead to a trackway and on to A286 south of Cocking. Here we are only 3 miles south of:

MIDHURST (SU8821). Access from north and south by A286 and from east and west by A272. Nearest station—Haslemere (8½m). E.C. Wed.

An ancient town on the Rother with many old buildings; a good centre for walks. *See*: stocks and pillory, *Spread Eagle* Hotel. *Visit*: Cowdray ruins and park (1m NE).

To the south of this last section of the Way in the triangle between A285 and A286 converging on Chichester, the topography of the dip slope is complex. The upper part of the slope terminates in less than two miles in the bluffs of Levin Down, Count Hill and High Down, cut off by a transverse valley running eastwards from Singleton (*See*: Weald and Downland Open Air Museum and Country Park) through Charlton and East Dean. 'It winds and twists', wrote Cobbett, 'amongst the hills, some higher and some lower, forming cross dells, inlets and ground in such variety of shapes that it is impossible to describe.' South again there is another upstanding hill block, of which the most notable summit, St Roche's Hill (675ft), is surmounted by the Trundle, one of the best known Sussex camps, which is an Iron Age fort built around the site of a neolithic causewayed camp. Modern radio masts help to destroy the atmosphere. The view embraces the South Downs from Butser Hill to Devil's Dyke, while beyond the Lavant rises Bow Hill, another famous prehistoric site. Near at hand we look down the length of the straight on Goodwood Racecourse to the east. Southwards is Goodwood Car Racing Track and beyond it the cathedral city of:

CHICHESTER (around SU8604). Access by A27 from east and west, A285 and A286 from the north. Main line railway station. E.C. Thurs.

The first building on this site was carried out by migrants from the Trundle. The Romans built one of their earliest cities here (Noviomagus), with Stane Street to provide the important connection to Londinium. Sections of the Roman walls are still standing with some towers, but the gates have gone. The name 'Chichester' dates from the Saxon occupation. The cathedral is Norman (early twelfth century). *See*: Cathedral (the separate bell tower is unique in Britain); town walls; Market Cross; Canon Gate (medieval); many interesting buildings. *Visit*: Fishbourne (Roman palace) (1½m W); Bosham (Chichester Harbour Area of Outstanding Natural Beauty) (3m W); Boxgrove Church ('the cathedral of parish churches in Sussex') (3m NE); Goodwood House and park

(3m NNE); the Trundle (3½m N); Weald and Downland Open
Air Museum and Country Park (5½m N); Bow Hill (5m NNW).

References
O.S. 1 inch Map Sheets 181, 182
O.S. 2½ inch Map Sheets TQ11, 01, SU91, 81

COCKING TO OLD WINCHESTER HILL

Cocking–South Harting (Bow Hill)–Buriton–Butser Hill
(Petersfield)–Old Winchester Hill. Routes onward

This section continues the physical characteristics of the last.
Again the complex topography of the dip slope extends the
interest in diversions from the shortest route. Linch Down is the
second highest point of the Sussex Downs.

The South Downs Way ends at present at the Hampshire border
between South Harting and Buriton but trackways can be
followed along the hills to Butser Hill, the highest point of the
range, and minor roads on towards Old Winchester Hill and
Winchester. In the course of time an extension of the Way already
under discussion may cover the whole distance. A connection
with the North Downs Way can be made by following a scarp
edge past Hawkley and Selborne.

From Cocking to South Harting is 6¾ miles; another 2¼ lead
to the Hampshire border giving a total of 9 miles for the Way in
this section and a grand total of 72 miles from Eastbourne.
Three and a half miles from the Hampshire border to Butser Hill
summit and a further 5½ miles on to Old Winchester Hill add
another 9 miles of pleasant going to the end of the Way.

After crossing A286 the South Downs Way climbs by trackway
over Cocking Down to Linch Down (814ft); though the summits
are open the woodland cover is sufficient in places to limit the
views. From the more open sites we can see Black Down with

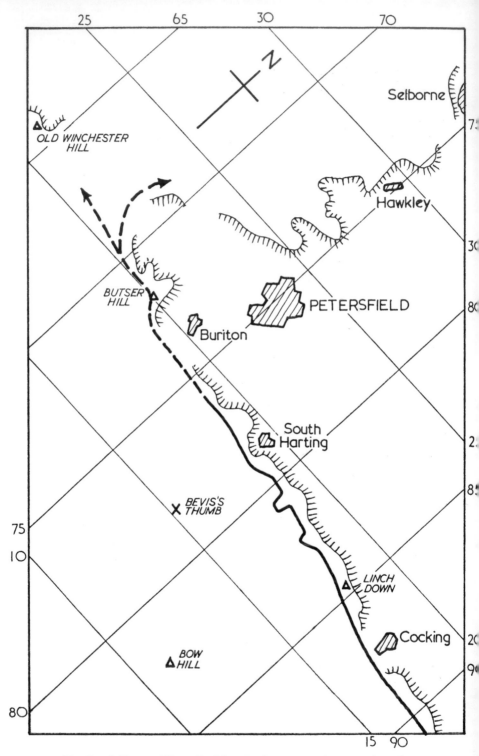

25   65   30   70

N

Selborne

OLD WINCHESTER
HILL

Hawkley

BUTSER
HILL

Buriton

PETERSFIELD

South
Harting

BEVIS'S
X THUMB

75

10

LINCH
DOWN

Cocking

BOW
△ HILL

80

15   90

13   South Downs Way: Cocking–Buriton, extensions north and west

Leith Hill and the chalk scars on the North Downs beyond, and opposite, Chichester Harbour and a glimpse of the Isle of Wight. A minor Roman road, northward bound from Noviomagus, crossed the ridge hereabouts. Didling Hill leads on to Treyford Hill (770ft); on its southern slopes is a line of five Bronze Age barrows known as the Devil's Humps. On the far side is a col 450ft above Treyford village.

The topography of the dip slopes is now complex. From this lowest point of the hills a dry valley runs south-eastwards through Chilgrove to join the Lavant close to Chichester. The western side of this valley rises to the great bluff of Bow Hill (677ft) only 5 miles from Chichester. It is a notable antiquarian site with the small circular camp of Goose Hill, four large round barrows of the Bronze Age (the Devil's Humps), a long barrow, various banks and entrenchments, field systems and trackways and the site of flint mines. Down below are the ancient yew trees, 'ghostly, fantastic and even bewitched', of Kingley Vale, a valley cutting deeply into the hills which is a National Nature Reserve.

Back on the main ridgeway we climb from the col to Beacon Hill (793ft). There are the remains of a rectangular camp, which the Way skirts on the south side. Hereabouts, possibly on the shoulder known as Telegraph Hill, there was a huge semaphore in the times of Napoleon, used to relay messages from Portsmouth towards London. Two miles to the south-west is another Tele-graph Hill, which may well have played a part in the same chain of communication. On its flanks is one of the outstanding long barrows of Sussex—Bevis's Thumb.

Soon B2141 comes in from the south-east, converging rapidly on the line of the scarp; the Way crosses Harting Down and descends to this road near its highest point. A short distance to the right a path branches off, skirting the northern slopes of Tower Hill to B2146 on the far side. In the wedge of country between these two roads are the house and grounds of the National Trust property of Uppark, which dates from the late seventeenth century. The roads plunge steeply down the scarp, joining before reaching the large village of South Harting (*See*: stocks and whipping post). The Way continues on the far side of B2146 by trackway on the flanks of the hills to end at the county boundary close to Sunwood Farm.

The trackways continue above the scarp. The main line railway to Portsmouth pierces the range below the Point 526, which we cross half a mile south of Buriton. Beyond is the minor road from Buriton to Rowland's Castle, which was formerly the main road from London to Portsmouth; a wooded hill of 801ft leads on to an underpass below the present-day main road (A3). At one time this threaded a steep-walled cutting through the Downs; now extensive grading and widening have completely changed the nature of the place so that the speeding motorist is hardly aware that he is passing through hill country. Two and a half miles north-east is:

PETERSFIELD (SU7423/24). Access by A3 from London and Portsmouth, A272 from east and west, A325 from the north. Main line railway station. E.C. Thurs.

See: Church (Norman) and old houses. *Visit*: Stoner Hill (2m NW), viewpoint.

From the A3 crossing we press on as rapidly as possible up the facing slopes of Butser Hill (888ft), the highest point of the South Downs, which radio masts and an access road have done much to tame. It is a massive hill and a worthy monarch, 'no fewer than eight spurs with almost headlong combes between them taper down from the circular plateau and make it the starfish of the southern hills'. Now there is a Country Park with a nature trail and a project to recreate a Stone Age village. Ramsdean Down is a prominent northerly shoulder; southwards Oxenbourne Down is the beginning of a ridge, crossed by A3, which leads on to Windmill Hill (633ft).

In ancient times the traveller westbound towards Winchester and Salisbury Plain left Butser Hill by the south-westerly ridge over Tegdown Hill and Hyden Hill with the scarp line still on his right hand. A little further on, the lesser trackway connecting this (the so-called South Hants Ridgeway) with the Lunway and the Harrow Way further north branched off over Wether Down. Though the lines of these routes have been painstakingly pieced together, they seldom provide footpath routes for walkers in the present-day countryside. Hereabouts the network of relatively minor roads has obliterated most of the story of the past.

If bound for Winchester therefore we are substantially committed to the hard going of these made-up roads on towards Old Winchester Hill (672ft). Two miles to the south is Broadhalfpenny Down where there is a memorial to the Hambledon Cricket Club, 1760–87. Old Winchester Hill carries a National Nature Reserve of 140 acres and a camp with single bank and ditch. A dozen miles of pleasantly rural Hampshire lead on to Winchester, which is overlooked on this side by a great camp on St Catherine's Hill.

From Winchester onwards there is no continuous walkers' route to the west. There is a north-facing scarp line starting at the Wiltshire border which can be followed along Dean Hill to the Pepperbox, a folly in the care of the National Trust, on A36. Now on the opposite side of the Avon is the Ox Drove Ridgeway.

The present-day rambler seeking a route to interconnect the South Downs Way and the North Downs Way will be drawn to the steep east-facing scarp edge of the Hampshire chalk block which runs northwards from Petersfield. The scarp face is often clothed with steep woods called hangers and it is not possible to follow easily a continuous route on or near the edge. However, minor roads are numerous. Wheatham Hill (813ft), 2½ miles from Petersfield, is a prominent salient ahead of the hill line with summit access by trackway. Beyond a sharp re-entrant is another outjutting hill above Hawkley. The hanger here was the scene of a landslide in 1774 when two houses and a barn were destroyed. William Cobbett in *Rural Rides* wrote of the view: 'it was like looking from the top of a castle down into the sea, except that the valley was land not water'. Next comes Hoar Hill (695ft) said

to be on the watershed between the North Sea and the English
Channel, followed by the celebrated Selborne Hanger above
Selborne, the home of Gilbert White the early naturalist. This
is a very attractive village and the hill scenery hereabouts is as
fine as any of the better known chalk districts.

There is one other ancient route westwards from this area—
the Lunway, which is largely lost at least in its early stages.
Hippisley Cox indicates a line west of Selborne, passing Oliver's
Battery earthwork (SU5836) and then north of Winchester.
Lunway Inn (SU5136) on A33 obviously fixes the line firmly at
that point. Timperley and Brill, whose scholarship is of course
more modern, suggest a line from the neighbourhood of Ellisfield
Camp (SU6245), which is near the Harrow Way, to Lunway Inn
on tracks and minor roads today. Crossing A33 the Lunway
continues on tracks for several miles, in fact almost all the way
to Stockbridge, passing Woolbury Ring, a 4 acre enclosure with
single bank and ditch, en route. After Stockbridge it coincides
with A30 and is of no interest to the walker.

There are however two more camps close to the route which
are worthy of notice. Danebury Hill (469ft), 3 miles north-west
of Stockbridge, is said by Hippisley Cox to rival Old Sarum—a
'square, sullen, beetling outline looking the very picture of a
savage stronghold'. There are three tiers of ramparts and a complex defended entrance. Close to Salisbury, less than half a mile
from A30 and the same distance away from the Roman road
from Old Sarum to Winchester, is Figsbury Ring, which belongs
to the National Trust. The area is 4 acres and there is a single
bank and ditch.

References
O.S. 1 inch Map Sheet 181 (to present end of path, also on to Old
    Winchester Hill and north to Selborne), 168, 167
O.S. 2½ inch Map Sheets SU81, 71 (to present end of path)
Leaflet Guides (Hampshire County Council)—*The Butser Trail*;
    The Danebury Trail
Leaflet Guide (Nature Conservancy)—*Old Winchester Hill Nature
    Trail*

Page 103
Fulking and
the South
Downs,
looking
west

Page 104
Freshwater
Stacks and
Tennyson
Down

5

THE ISLE OF WIGHT
AND SOUTH DORSET RIDGEWAYS

THE ISLE OF WIGHT RIDGEWAYS

Culver Cliff–Brading–Newport–Carisbrooke–Brighstone
Down–Freshwater–Tennyson Down–The Needles
Shanklin–St Boniface Down–St Catherine's Point

THE Isle of Wight, 23 miles long and 13 miles wide, roughly diamond shaped, stands athwart Southampton Water, separated from the mainland by the famous channels of the Solent to the west and Spithead to the east. It is all that remains of the south wall of the valley of the one-time Solent River which continued the line of the Frome to a mouth somewhere in the neighbourhood of the present-day Spithead. We know that the land extended much further south at one time because the valleys of the south-flowing rivers are more extensive than is warranted by the scale of the present streams. This land was slowly eroded from the south, the sea breaking finally through the valley wall and flooding it. The facing chalk ridges at the Foreland by Swanage and the Needles at the west end of the island were once connected by a ridge now dispersed over the bed of the Channel.

The chalk ridges of the island were formed during the Alpine folding at the same time as the others in the South East. The island exhibits the same erosion phenomena as, for example, the Weald. In the chalk ridge running from the Needles to Culver Cliff the tilt of the beds is such that scarp and dip slopes are equally steep. It corresponds to the North Downs, the chalk sinking to the north beneath the newer rocks of the Hampshire Basin, just as that of the North Downs sinks below those of the London Basin. There was a dome here, as over the Weald, and the streams running from it cut down progressively through the chalk to form

G

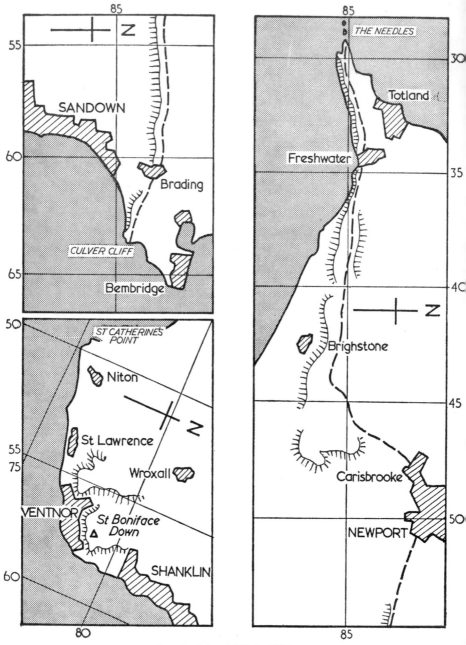

14 The Isle of Wight Ridgeways

the gaps, which are such a feature of the landscape today. Thus the gaps formed by the East and West Yar and the Medina correspond to those of the Wey, the Mole, the Darent and the Medway, and there are analogous towns guarding the gaps.

The southernmost tip of the island is the remains of another chalk ridge, corresponding perhaps to the South Downs; the one-time extent and outline is now difficult to determine. It is important however, in providing the highest point—St Boniface Down (785ft), and the background ridge and cliffs above the famous landslip area around Ventnor. Between the two chalk ridges we find the other rocks of the Weald succession.

There are no Countryside Commission routes on the island, but the County Council has prepared a magnificent series of long-distance trails, which are described in a series of special leaflets. The trails are waymarked in red and there are signposts at key junctions. For the main chalk ridge we start at Culver Cliff and join the Bembridge Trail just beyond the Brading Gap. This leads to Shide by Newport. From Carisbrooke beyond the Medina Gap the Tennyson Trail is continuous to the Needles in the far west. The other trails, notably the Worsley Trail, touch on the chalk in places but are traverses rather than ridgeway routes.

From Culver Cliff to Newport the ridgeway route is 13 miles, mostly on minor roads. The Bembridge Trail gives a footpath and trackway alternative on one side or the other of the ridge. The Tennyson Trail from Carisbrooke to Alum Bay is 15 miles. On the southern ridge Shanklin to St Catherine's Point will be, perhaps, 8 miles.

We start at Culver Cliff, an impressive chalk headland to the north of Sandown Bay. Whitecliff Bay on its north side has features similar to those of Alum Bay at the far end of the island. A minor road along the top leads over Bembridge Down to B3395. This is followed steeply downhill to Brading, a gap village on the East Yar, said to be the oldest town with the oldest church and the oldest houses on the island. There is a Roman villa, also a wax museum. The route onwards on the ridge top is minor road all the way to Newport, the Bembridge Trail is to the north at first, later to the south. We climb Brading Down, leaving Nunwell House (sometimes open to the public) away to the north, cross Ashley Down with its prominent seamark at 450ft and continue along Arreton Down. The views are far reaching and include the sea both north and south. The Bembridge Trail, here to the south, passes close to Arreton Manor, which is sometimes open to the public. Both routes come eventually to Shide in the Medina Gap on the south side of:

NEWPORT (SZ49/5088/89). Access by A3020 from Cowes and Shanklin/Ventnor, A3056 from Sandown, A3054 from Ryde, B3401 and B3323 from the south-west. E.C. Thurs.

County town, on the River Medina. *See*: Carisbrooke Castle, built on the remains of a Roman fort, where Charles I was imprisoned for a time (shell keep, donkey-driven well etc); Roman villa. *Visit*: Osborne House (4m N); Cowes (4½m N).

The ridgeway route now follows the Tennyson Trail westwards starting in Carisbrooke at O.S. ref 482881. The Trail climbs to Point 407 and on south-westwards along Bowcombe Down. Less than a mile to the west is the Rowridge Television Station and mast. At Idlecombe Down we swing round towards the west and make for Brighstone Forest, which is traversed to the open slopes of Brighstone Down (702ft). The view is a particularly wide one, embracing Culver Cliff on the one hand, and past St Catherine's to Freshwater and Tennyson Down on the other. We reach the minor road which connects Calbourne and Brighstone; there is a Roman villa a short distance down towards the latter, the former has a famous water-mill and an ancient church. The Trail continues along Mottistone Down; below to the south are the Long Stone, a single standing stone dating from 2000–3000 BC, and a sixteenth-century manorhouse at Mottistone. The views once again are extensive.

Next comes B3399, between Brighstone and Freshwater, which

crosses the ridge at a col (306ft). The way continues immediately opposite over Point 538, followed by Brook Down and Afton Down. Now the coastline is converging rapidly and eventually we join the coastal footpath for a descent to Freshwater, a gap village where the north-flowing West Yar almost cuts the island in two. Freshwater Bay has chalk cliffs and caves to the west and two fine stacks (the Arch and the Stag) to the east. Beyond the village the path climbs Tennyson Down, which is a National Trust property. At the summit is a monument to the poet who for some years lived and worked at Farringford House down below. The granite cross is 38ft high. Now the island narrows rapidly. The south coast below the Down and on towards the Needles is a magnificent series of very steep chalk cliffs, with some pinnacles and caves below, culminating in the glories of Scratchell's Bay. Unfortunately we are cut off now from viewing this by a fatuously sited experimental rocket range. We are excluded, too, by the Coastguard Service from the highlight of this promontory—the chalk stacks of the Needles. The nearest glimpse we can get from the land of this piece of our coastal heritage is through a barbed-wire fence at a range of about half a mile. There are three teeth, some 80ft high, and at the outward end a lighthouse on a reef at sea level. The name came from a large slender needle-like pillar, 180ft high, which fell late in the eighteenth century. 'Now,' explained a guide-book soon afterwards, 'they appear more like wedges set on their bases, or the ragged grinders of an enormous jaw, than the instrument from which they receive their name.' Fifteen miles ahead the chalk stacks of Old Harry and His Wife beside Swanage mark the one-time line of the chalk ridge on which we stand. For a nearer view of the Needles and the other pinnacles and the caves hereabouts, a boat trip round the promontory might be the most fitting conclusion to our trip from Culver Cliff.

To the north the variegated coloured sands of Alum Bay make this an alternative place of pilgrimage, well equipped to handle such travellers. The paths from the ridge top run easily down on this side.

The more southerly chalk block rises very close to the coast, the steep slope on its seaward side sheltering Bonchurch, Ventnor and St Lawrence and giving them a very pleasing micro-climate. This is landslip country similar to the Warren at Folkstone, Under Hooken at Beer, and so on. The coast road and the houses are built on the undercliff; chalk is exposed in steep crags at various places a short way inland; above the crags are the chalk hills. At the ends beyond Blackgang Chine in the west and Luccombe Chine in the east, the cliffs show outcrops of the other Wealden rocks.

From Shanklin various footpaths lead to Shanklin Down (773ft) and the ridge is then followed to Hanger Hill above Bonchurch, then somewhat south of west to St Boniface Down (785ft) above Ventnor, the summit of the island. There is road access to this point, but the actual peak is enclosed in the wire fence of a Government Radio Station and is not accessible. The masts complete the devastation of a noble hill.

The Worsley Trail runs somewhat further north, from Shanklin Down over the shoulder of St Martin's Down and descends to Wroxall. The Stenbury Trail coming from Ventnor over Rew Down to Week Down follows this ridge and then descends into the valley of the East Yar.

To continue our way on the chalk it is best to go from Week Down over Rew Down to the edge of the landslip and to follow this, with great views out over the undercliff and the sea, to A3055 by Niton. The road swings inland to Niton village, but there are footpath lines, which are shorter, above St Catherine's Point and lighthouse to Blackgang Chine and so to St Catherine's Hill (773ft). This is topped by an ancient lighthouse which dates back to the fourteenth century; the present lighthouse was sited at a much lower level in 1840 for the usual reasons. This is the seaward end of yet another ridge stretching northwards along St Catherine's Down to the so-called Alexandrian Pillar, 70ft high, which commemorates the visit of Alexander I of Russia in 1814.

As far as chalk is concerned the whole walk is of merely local interest. The most sensible extension would be to take the coast path after Blackgang Chine past Whale Chine and Shepherd's Chine to join the Tennyson Trail by Freshwater. This crosses a succession of Wealden beds between the two chalk ridges many of which are exposed on the cliffs. A similar succession can be sought between the other end of the chalk ridges between Bonchurch and Culver Cliff, but here the extensive building over of Shanklin and Sandown tends to obscure the details.

References
O.S. 1 inch Map Sheet 180
O.S. 2½ inch Map Sheets SU38, 48, 58, 68, 47, 57
Leaflet Guides (Isle of Wight County Council, 1971)—*Bembridge Trail* (Bembridge Point to Newport); *Hamstead Trail* (Brook Bay to Hamstead Ledge); *Nunwell Trail* (Sandown to Ryde); *Shepherd's Trail* (Shepherd's Chine to Carisbrooke); *Stenbury Trail* (Ventnor to Newport); *Tennyson Trail* (Carisbrooke to Alum Bay); *Worsley Trail* (Shanklin to Brighstone Forest); *Coastal Path*

THE FORELAND TO BEAMINSTER DOWN
The Foreland–Studland–Swanage–Corfe–East and West Lulworth–Durdle Door–White Nothe–Ringstead Bay–Weymouth Dorchester–Maiden Castle–Hardy Monument (Abbotsbury) Eggardon Camp–Powerstock–Beaminster Down

This ridgeway with many fine views of the sea in its nearly fifty miles is inextricably bound up with the South-West Peninsula Coast Path. The starting point by the pinnacles at the Foreland is on the coastal route and they share the first mile of cliff to Ballard Down. The chalkway now follows the Purbeck Hill ridge towards and beyond Corfe, while the other departs southwards. Whether you come by hill-ridge or cliff-top the great range at Tyneham cares nought for intentions, for neither route is permissible. The cliffs are completely inaccessible; the road on the hill-top is lined with high barbed fences and soon guides the traveller down the northern scarp to East Lulworth. Sometimes there is no thoroughfare even here and a wide detour has to be made by Wareham. Only beyond Lulworth Cove can the natural routes be resumed, running thenceforward hand-in-hand over great chalk cliffs to White Nothe. Now the coastway divides into a coast hugging route through Weymouth and alongside Chesil Bank and an inland route on the hills to the north. The chalkway follows the latter, coming back to the sea again by Abbotsbury. The ridgeway traveller branches off at the Hardy Monument and crossing A35 proceeds through quiet country to Eggardon Camp and on north-westwards to the Great Ridgeway at Beaminster Down.

The many sea views make the walking of this ridgeway an outstanding experience; while the camps at Maiden Castle and Eggardon are among the most impressive in the country.

The Foreland to Corfe is 6½ miles and East Lulworth is a further 7 miles. Eight miles lead on to Ringstead Bay, from which it is 7 miles to Ridgeway Hill on the Dorchester to Weymouth road. Here Maiden Castle is 1½ miles north. Continuing the Ridgeway 4 miles bring us to the Hardy Monument and another 4 to Abbotsbury Castle. Turning off at the Hardy Monument it is 7½ miles to Eggardon Camp and a further 7½ miles to the Great Ridgeway on Beaminster Down—a total of 47½ miles.

The Foreland, otherwise Handfast Point, separating Poole Bay from Swanage Bay, looks across the open sea to a kindred headland at the west end of the Isle of Wight. These headlands, which were once connected, both have their chalk pinnacles, there the famous Needles, here Old Harry and Old Harry's Wife. Away to the north-east the skyscrapers of Bournemouth loom above the sandy cliffs. The path (also here the South-West Peninsula Coast Path) follows the cliff edge to Ballard Point passing on the way a series of fine chalk buttresses, off-shore pinnacles known as the Haystack and the Pinnacle and the caves, not readily identifiable, of Parson's Barn and Little Barn. The

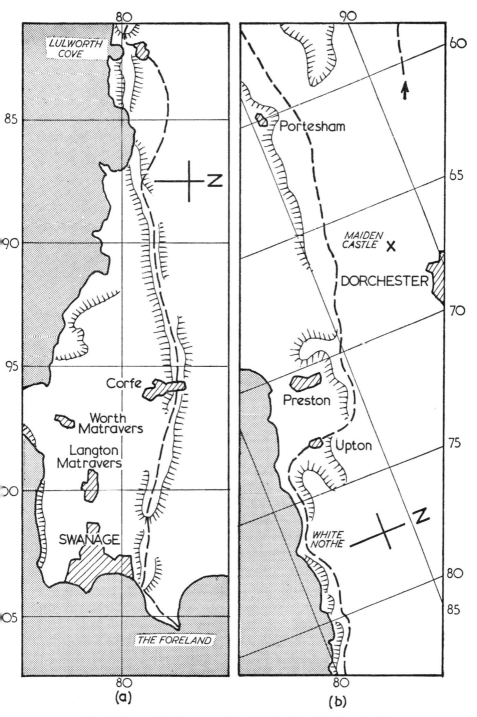

15 South Dorset Ridgeways: (a) The Foreland–Lulworth Cove;
(b) Lulworth Cove–Abbotsbury

ridgeway now turns west along Ballard Down and we look southwards to

SWANAGE (SZ02/0378/79). Access by A351 from Wareham and via Sandbanks–South Haven Point ferry. Nearest station—Wareham (10m). Youth Hostel. E.C. Thurs.

The town was mentioned in the Domesday Book. A fishing port in Leland's time, later the centre of the local quarrying industry, now a thriving resort with a sandy beach. *See*: Old Lock-up. *Visit*: Peveril Point; Durlston Head, the Globe and Tilly Whim Caves (1m S); Anvil Point Lighthouse (1m S); Ballard Down (1m N); the Foreland (2m NE)

and northwards to

STUDLAND (SZ0382). Access by B3351 from A351 and by minor road from Swanage. Ferry from South Haven Point to Sandbanks by Bournemouth. Nearest station—Wareham (10m). E.C. Thurs.

Pretty village with sandy beach. *Visit*: The Foreland (1m E); the Agglestone ($\frac{1}{2}$m W), an isolated sandstone boulder which gives a few short climbs.

Once on the ridge there are wide views southwards to the limestone hills and the sea, northwards across the heathlands to Poole Harbour. In 2 miles the Swanage to Studland road crosses at a col, beyond which the narrow ridge climbs higher over Godlingston Hill and Nine Barrow Down (654ft).

Three miles ahead Corfe stands at a gap worn in the chalk by streams flowing from the south draining a valley between here and the limestone. The Corfe River continues across the heathlands to Poole Harbour. Surmounting a sculpted knoll in the gap are the magnificent ruins of Corfe Castle on a site said by Braun to be 'as fine as any in this country'. There was an outstanding keep.

The fragmentary nature of the present-day remains is the result of a thorough 'slighting' by Oliver Cromwell after he captured it in the Civil War.

Beyond the gap the hill-line climbs again by West Hill and Knowle Hill, where a minor road crosses, followed by Ridgeway Hill with Grange Arch. This was erected to 'complete the view' from Creech Grange which lies below Great Wood on the northern slopes of the ridge. The house and gardens are open to the public. The sea is accessible at Kimmeridge Bay, 2 miles to the south, but this is on the edge of the Tyneham Range and there is no coastal route on westwards. Soon our chalk ridge route leads out to a road, where a leftward turn, open at only infrequent intervals in the summer, can be taken to the scenic splendours of Worbarrow Bay. (This is all range area and the road must be strictly followed.) The hill top route continues between high fences and then plunges abruptly down the scarp on the north side to East Lulworth. The castle here was almost completely destroyed by fire in 1929 and only a shell remains. We continue, by road unfortunately, through the drabness of Lulworth Camp to West Lulworth and Lulworth Cove.

WEST LULWORTH (SY8280). Access by B3071 from Wool on A352. Nearest station—Wool (4½m). E.C. Wed.

Lulworth Cove is a small perfectly shaped natural harbour, formed where the sea has breached the limestone wall and hollowed out softer strata behind. Stair Hole, nearby, shows the same process in a less advanced state. There are caves and on the east side of the bay is the famous forest.

On the far side the next hill is Hanbury Tout. Here chalk hills and limestone cliffs are still separated by a narrow valley, through which we climb up and up to the top of Dungy Head. Above St Oswald's Bay is a large caravan park. The path continues on the cliff-top though there are straightforward ways down to the beach for anyone wishing to take a closer look at the imposing limestone arch of Durdle Door. This beach is dominated by the great chalk headland of Swyre. Bat's Head, further on, is holed at sea-level; the opening which is known as the Eye of the Monster is an impressive sight at sunset viewed from the easterly side. At West Bottom, three quarters of a mile ahead, is a semi-cylindrical buttress of chalk, 300ft high, known as Fountain Rock, which carries near the summit a stone with an inscription to Llewelyn Powys, the local author. The sides of the rock are banded with horizontal lines of flint. In due course we reach the culminating chalk headland of White Nothe, surmounted by a row of disused coastguard cottages. The route continues gently down to Ringstead Bay, passing Burning Cliff, so called from an incident in the 1820s when iron pyrites ignited an outcrop of oil shales which continued to smoulder for four years. Beyond is a cluster of radio masts.

Hereabouts we have to leave the coastline and follow the chalk hills inland. This route is a variation of the South-West Peninsula Coast Path, introduced as an alternative to urban Weymouth and the inner bank of the Fleet behind Chesil Beach. Trackways lead north and then west over Moign Down and, crossing A353 at Upton, continue up White Horse Hill, named for a huge figure of George III on horseback, 280ft long and 323ft high, which was cut in 1808 on the south facing scarp above Sutton Poyntz. A minor road is crossed at Green Hill, close to the Iron Age Chalbury Camp, a single bank and ditch with pit dwellings. Of the valley below Pitt-Rivers has written: 'To pass through Chalbury at twilight, shut in by the ridge hills, seeing the long tombs cut against the afterglow, is to experience an almost unnerving feeling of the latent force of the past.'

After Bincombe, the road (A354) and railway from Dorchester to Weymouth are crossed at Ridgeway Hill. Three miles north is:

DORCHESTER (SY68/6989/90). Access from east and west by A35, by A354 from Blandford Forum and Weymouth and by

A37 from the north-west. Main line railway station. E.C.
Thurs.

The county town of Dorset standing on an ancient site, the
Roman Durnovaria. Within the town are the Roman remains
of a camp (Poundbury) and an amphitheatre (Maumbury
Rings), later used for public executions. A series of disastrous
fires destroyed most of the old town during the eighteenth
and nineteenth centuries. It is 'Casterbridge' of the Thomas
Hardy novels. *See*: Museum; old houses and inns. *Visit*:
Maiden Castle (1½m SW).

The same distance south of the A354 crossing is:

WEYMOUTH (SY66 to 68/76 to 80). Access by A353 (east), A354
(north) and B3157 (west). Main line railway station. Information Bureau. E.C. Wed.

The history goes back to the fourteenth century. Formerly
Weymouth and Melcombe Regis were separate towns on
either side of the River Wey. In Leland's time there was no
bridge but a boat attached to a swinging rope: 'In the ferry
boote they used no ores.' The importance of Weymouth as a
watering place dates from the reign of George III. Now it is a
substantial resort with sandy beaches facing east and south-
east. There is a modern port with steamer services to the
Channel Islands. To the south between here and Portland is
the naval anchorage of Portland Harbour. *See*: Piers and
Harbour; Radipole Lake; Sandsfoot Castle. *Visit*: Isle of
Portland (2½m S); Chesil Beach (2m SW); the White Horse
(5m NNE); Chalbury Camp (4½m NNE).

Crossing A354 we continue by a trackway opposite in half a mile
to B3159. One and a half miles to the north is Maiden Castle, the
greatest British earthwork. It was occupied from Neolithic times
and continuously enlarged. The present pattern is an oval 400yd
by 900yd; there are never less than three separate lines of defence

with the entrance gaps in the 40ft banks ingeniously staggered. The perimeter is 2 miles so that a large force would have been needed for successful defence. A notable event was its capture by the Romans under Vespasian in AD 43–4. The central area has never been ploughed and the present vegetation is due to centuries of sheep-grazing. Now new suburbs of Dorchester are creeping slowly across the flat fields towards the earthwork, an enemy far more menacing than it has known before.

Hereabouts one could strike off northwards, crossing A35 and the River Frome, perhaps by Bradford Peveril, and so join the Furzy Down Way, which leads up the ridge between the Cerne and Sydling valleys to the Great Ridgeway close to Batcombe.

Back on the South Dorset Ridgeway we continue over Great Hill and Bronkham Hill and climb finally to the Hardy Monument, which rises on Black Down (776ft) beside a minor road from Martinstown to Abbotsbury. It has commemorated since 1844 Nelson's Trafalgar colleague who lived nearby at Portisham. Variously described as 'a grey wide-mouthed factory chimney' or as 'a telephone receiver standing on end' it commands a wide view from White Nothe to Golden Cap, as well as over the inland hills.

Here now the main chalk way parts from the South-West Peninsula Coast Path. The latter passes close to Hell Stone, a dolmen of nine upright stones re-erected in the last century, the head of the Valley of Stones leading down to Littlebredy and the stone circle of 'Grey Mare and her Colts'; then on over White Hill and Wears Hill to the triangular earthwork of Abbotsbury Castle. Below to the south is:

ABBOTSBURY (SY5785). On B3157 between Bridport and Weymouth. Nearest station—Weymouth (9m). E.C. Thurs.

Only fragments remain of a monastery of the eleventh century. *See*: Church; Abbey Barn (reed thatched); the Swannery—the largest in Europe dating from Saxon times; sub-tropical Gardens; St Catherine's Chapel on a 250ft hill beside the sea. *Visit*: Chesil Beach (1m SW).

From the Hardy Monument the chalkway line runs north crossing A35 at Winterbourne Abbas and climbing out on the far side on to the hills again. Along the top runs the Roman road from Dorchester to the west; a present-day minor road follows the same line to Eggardon Camp, strikingly situated on a spur jutting into the valley of the Brit. The area is 20 acres; there are three ramparts on each of the three sides, the fourth is divided from the hill by a narrow neck with two ramparts. Second only to Maiden Castle among Wessex earthworks, this is threatened at the present time with television masts and other eye-catching scenic improvements! North-westerly in the valley below is Powerstock, where the earthworks are the worthy remains of a Norman motte-and-bailey castle.

Eggardon Camp is only some seven miles from the Great Ridgeway on Beaminster Down. Though there is no obvious walking line over this distance, it is a quiet countryside. Alternatively a route can be sought towards Maiden Newton to join the southern loop of the Great Ridgeway which crosses the River Frome close by Cattistock.

References
O.S. 1 inch Map Sheets 177, 178, 179
O.S. 2½ inch Map Sheets SZ08, SY98, 88, 78, 68, 59, 58, 49, ST40

6

THE GREAT RIDGEWAY

WESTERN SECTION: AXMOUTH TO TOLLER DOWN GATE

This section, though not on chalk, is accorded brief mention because it forms part of the ancient lengthy ridgeway route of nearly 300 miles which extended from here to the Wash.

From the sea at Axmouth to Toller Down Gate on the Dorchester–Crewkerne road it is 23 miles, mostly on minor roads looking out over the Marshwood Vale.

Reference
O.S. 1 inch Map Sheet 177

WESTERN SECTION: TOLLER DOWN GATE TO SALISBURY PLAIN

*Toller Down Gate–Evershot–Holywell–Batcombe Hill
Gore Hill–High Stoy–Dogbury Camp–Little Minterne Hill
Church Hill–Ball Hill–Nettlecombe Tout–Dorsetshire Gap
Bulbarrow Hill–Bell Hill–Hambledon and Hod Hills
Smugglers' Lane–Ashmore Down–Win Green Hill
Shaftesbury–East Knoyle–Sutton Veney–Bishopstow–Boreham*

In this section the route runs for much of the way on top of a north-facing scarp, looking out over Blackmoor Vale to the Mendips and other Somerset hills, but it is true ridgeway country for often equally extensive views open up to the south. From Toller Down Gate onwards all is now chalk. A substantial part is on hill-top trackways rather than roads, in fact in the 23 miles between Dogbury Gate on A352 and the old Blandford Forum to Shaftesbury road by Everley Hill Farm only some five miles are made-up roadways.

120

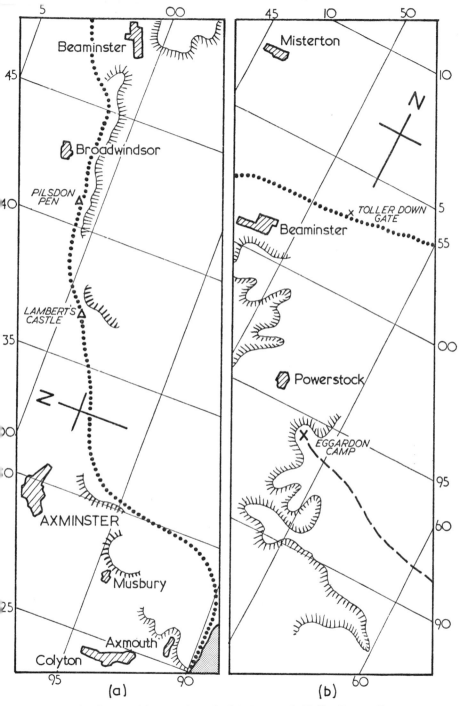

16 The Great Ridgeway (West): (a) Axmouth–Toller Down Gate;
(b) connections with South Dorset Ridgeways

There is a gap in the chalk scarp between Shillingstone Hill and Hambledon and Hod Hills cut by the River Stour flowing south-eastwards towards Poole Harbour. Beyond this break the scarp line runs northerly to Shaftesbury with fine hill bastions and combes facing west to Blackmoor Vale. This is the edge of a block of chalk country known as Cranborne Chase stretching towards the sea between the valleys of the Stour and the Avon, sliding down eventually below the sands of the Hampshire Basin. It is bounded in the north by the valley of the Ebble, while Win Green Hill (910ft) in its north-west corner is the highest point.

Toller Down Gate to Holywell is 5 miles, then Dogbury Gate on A352 is 4½ miles and Folly a further 5 miles. Past the Dorset-shire Gap and on up Bulbarrow Hill is 5 miles and a further 5 miles lead to Shillingstone on A357. Over Hambledon Hill to the crossing of A350 is 3½ miles, whence 9 miles mostly on roads take us to Win Green Hill. From here it is 19 road miles to Boreham on the edge of Salisbury Plain.

On A356 at Toller Down Gate are the ancient Hore Stones. We are faced with the problem of how the Great Ridgeway crossed the River Frome. To stay on the chalk the crossing would have to be further south between Cattistock Camp and Maiden Newton, but there are no footpaths to persuade the present-day traveller in this direction. The obvious modern way, which may in fact have acted as a fair weather alternative in earlier times, is not on the chalk, passing by Benville to Evershot, Holywell and returning again to the chalk at Batcombe Hill. It has the advantage of passing Benville Bridge which, in common with some others in the county, carries a plaque with an act of George IV:

'Any person wilfully INJURING any part of this COUNTY BRIDGE will be guilty of FELONY and upon conviction liable to be TRANSPORTED FOR LIFE by the court' FOOKS

Nowadays, of course, there is nowhere left to send them. Passing Evershot with some fine old houses we reach A37 at Holywell.

The Great Ridgeway sweeps round the head of Batcombe on a minor road with distant views north and south. We pass Cross and Hand, a stone pillar, said (recalling Ralph's Cross on the Yorkshire Moors) to have been a receptacle for alms for passing wayfarers. From Gore Hill (863ft) 6 miles of unmetalled trackway lead down towards Dorchester, once called the Furzy Down Way. Indeed the pattern here is of a series of southward stretching hill ridges with valleys like those of Up Sydling and Up Cerne between. Some of them carry roads, but this particular ridge has escaped that fate. The traveller visiting Cerne Abbas to see the chalk-cut giant, the medieval houses and the slight remains of the abbey could well turn off down the next valley leading to Up Cerne. The prodigious giant on the west-facing hillside above the village, 180ft high, is probably a Romano-British figure of Hercules.

The Great Ridgeway continues along Telegraph Hill and crosses A352 at Dogbury Gate. Now starts the best section of the route for walkers. Climbing south-eastwards up the crest of Little Minterne Hill, we cross the old Dorchester to Sherborne road and follow an easterly branch ridge to B3143 between Henley and Alton Pancras. Two miles of trackway continue over Church Hill and Ball Hill (825ft) to the house which used to be an inn at Folly on the Mappowder to Piddletrenthide road. The next hill, tree-crowned, is Nettlecombe Tout, jutting out and conspicuous from afar; we traverse it to a striking cleft in the ridge called the Dorsetshire Gap. The surrounding woods, as Timperley and Brill point out, destroy the effect which the Gap might otherwise have particularly when viewed from Blackmoor Vale. Early Ordnance Survey maps indicate that many trackways crossed the ridge here at one time, but it is an all too minor feature nowadays.

The route taken by the Ridgeway to reach the slopes of Bulbarrow Hill opposite is completely unknown. The aim is to reach the road which climbs the south ridge of the hill from Ansty Cross; there are a number of possibilities, the most direct being by way of Breach Wood. Sooner or later comes a road section up the long shoulder of Bulbarrow Hill (901ft), the summit inaccessible in a triangle of roads and disfigured by an unpleasant collection of radio masts and remains of war-time hutments. Nevertheless the huge view, particularly from north round to west, makes it a place of great interest from which cars could not easily be excluded under present circumstances. The remains of Rawlsbury Camp grace a westerly shoulder close to the Hazelbury Bryan road.

The Great Ridgeway follows the road which swings round the huge embayment of Woolland Hill. After 2 miles this slopes steeply down the scarp to Belchowell Street, but we continue at high level by trackway over Bell Hill to the minor road between Okeford Fitzpaine and Winterbourne Strickland; then on again by more trackway through Forestry Commission land until a path in a steep break in the woodlands leads down towards Shillingstone. Here now is the Stour Gap. Opposite rise Hambledon Hill and Hod Hill each surmounted by a camp; near at hand the northern slopes of Shillingstone Hill are scarred by a huge quarry.

Here again we do not know exactly where the Great Ridgeway crossed the valley. Timperley and Brill favour the route by Alder's Coppice to Hanford House, which the Ordnance Survey shows as fording the river at 839106. A mile upstream another ford is shown leading to Little Hanford, but the modern traveller may prefer to cross at Hayward Bridge on the road leading to Child Okeford. While it seems certain that the ancient way followed the col between Hod and Hambledon Hills, it is worthwhile at this point to climb over the latter for the sake of the magnificent Neolithic camp with which it is crowned. The ditch on this 622ft summit has a circumference of 2 miles. There was action here during the Civil War, when a local rising under the Rector of Compton led to a storming of the hill by Parliamentary troops under Colonel Desborough. Hod Hill (470ft) a mile away also has a hill-top camp, smaller but with a Roman fort occupying 7 acres in one corner. These two hills are outliers, separated from the main scarp of the chalk by the Iwerne river. Four miles south-east is:

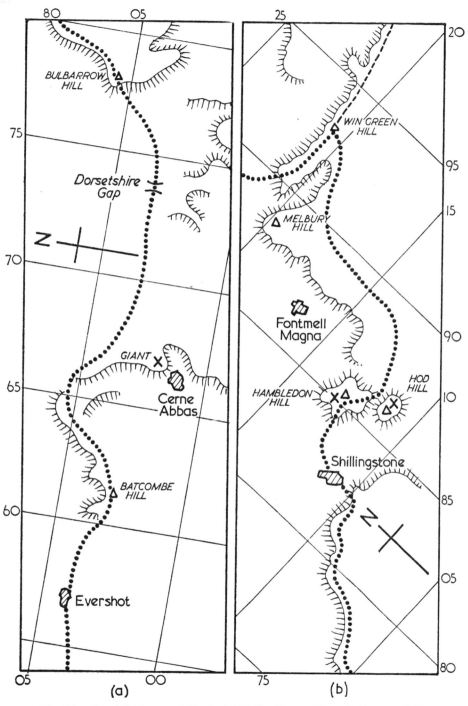

17 The Great Ridgeway (West): (a) Toller Down Gate–Bulbarrow Hill;
(b) Bulbarrow Hill–Win Green Hill

BLANDFORD FORUM (ST88/8906/07). Access by A354 from the north-east and south-west and by A350 from north-west and south-east. Nearest station—Wimborne Minster (11m). E.C. Wed.

A pleasant town beside the Stour with interesting old houses. *Visit*: Pimperne Long Barrow (2½m NE); Buzbury Rings (1½m E); Badbury Rings (5m ESE); Hambledon and Hod Hills (3½m NW).

Beyond the Iwerne river the scarp line turns north and runs up to Shaftesbury with some fine spurs and embayments above Blackmoor Vale. We are soon able to leave the main road and to proceed north-eastwards by the ancient Smugglers' Lane, now a somewhat desolate trackway climbing in a thin belt of trees. In a mile and a half comes the old Blandford to Shaftesbury road, which follows the line once taken by the Great Ridgeway. It is too busy for walking comfort and the problem is to leave it as soon as possible. Certainly there is a trackway beyond Iwerne Hill leading towards Ashmore, but it may well be possible to find a more circuitous and more pleasant route even further east. The prehistoric way almost certainly continued on the present road as far as Fontmell Down before turning east-south-east and climbing Ashmore Down. Hereabouts the outjutting spur of Melbury Hill (862ft) is a typical bare chalk summit commanding a splendid view.

Whatever our route we finish on B3081, the road from Tollard Royal to Shaftesbury, which at Charlton Down runs out on to the summit of a north-facing scarp above the headwaters of the Nadder and Ebble rivers. Turning right and still climbing we come in half a mile to Win Green Hill (910ft), a 360 degree view-point, the highest point of Cranborne Chase. The summit carries a character-giving clump of trees; in spite of the horseflies it is one of the outstanding chalk hills of the south.

At this point we turn aside to look at some of the interesting antiquities of Cranborne Chase. From the neighbourhood of Blandford Forum an ancient route once ran down towards the sea at Christchurch. This passed close to Pimperne Long Barrow (9110), Buzbury Rings (9105/06) and came to the magnificent circular camp of Badbury Rings (9602/03). There are three tiers of banks and ditches, the middle bank 40ft high, enclosing an area of 14 acres, with a dense clump of trees in the centre. King Arthur's soul inhabits a raven's body here until he is ready 'to come again to rule once more'. 'A magic bird in a haunted wood,' says Michael Pitt-Rivers, 'an ancient cliff washed by a sea changed to earth.' Originally a Stone Age fort, it was occupied in turn by Celtic invaders and then used by the Romans as a centre of their road system. From here the Roman Ackling Dyke ran north-eastwards towards Old Sarum. Still traceable over a distance of many miles, slowly converging on the A354 just short of Woodyates, it is among the finest examples of Roman road in Britain.

Immediately north of Woodyates is Bokerly Ditch, an earthwork boundary dating to the fourth century AD. It is some four miles long and blocked entry into the Chase from the direction of Salisbury. The county boundary still runs along it. Nearby, too, is another archaeological curiosity, the Dorset Cursus, over six miles of parallel banks with outside ditches—the function is no longer clear. Processional or funeral ways, race-tracks? The meaning is lost to us, only the shapes remain. There are many other lesser sites and in fact this country will have great appeal for the traveller with an interest in the ways of ancient man.

The line of the Great Ridgeway onwards to Salisbury Plain can be delineated though it is in fact almost all on roads and of little interest to the walker. From Win Green Hill it descends over Charlton Down and Zig Zag Hill to Cann Common and Shaftesbury.

SHAFTESBURY (ST85/8622/23). Access by A30 from east and west and by A350 from north and south. Nearest station— Semley (2½m NNE). E.C. Wed.

A hill town finely situated at 700ft looking out over Black-moor Vale. Reputedly Saxon, though most of it is much more recent. *See*: the famous cobbled Gold Hill; St Peter's Church (medieval); Museum.

The Great Ridgeway followed the present A350 northwards for some nine miles through East Knoyle to Pertwood. An alternative route by tracks and minor roads via Castle Rings, Semley and Hindon would seem preferable for the walker. The Harrow Way crosses here on the line of A303, the Grovely Ridgeway crosses a little further north. There is a short section on tracks over Little-combe and Whiten Hills before we descend through Sutton Veney to Bishopstow and Boreham on the Wylye. Salisbury Plain rises on the far bank.

References
O.S. 1 inch Map Sheets 166, 167, 177, 178
O.S. 2½ inch Map Sheets ST50, 60, 70, 80, 81, 82, 83, 84, 91, 92, 93, 94

EASTERN SECTION: THE WASH TO IVINGHOE BEACON HILL

The most northerly chalk in the country is in the East Riding of Yorkshire. Starting at the huge sea cliffs of Bempton and Flam-borough the outcrop swings round in an arc to the Humber. One day a long distance footpath—the Wolds Way—will serve this section.

The outcrop continues through Lincolnshire until cut off again by the Wash. On the far side south-eastern chalk begins at Hunstanton; somewhere hereabouts the Great Ridgeway terminated its long journey from Devon. Nowadays the modern traveller follows the line of the ancient Peddar's Way (also scheduled to become a long distance footpath in the course of time).

From Holme-next-the-Sea the line is very nearly straight through Fring to Castle Acre (20 miles), where the whole village lies inside the bailey of the former castle. There is a large mound with some slight remains. Nearby are the impressive ruins of the eleventh-century priory with a fine Tudor gateway. There are priory ruins also at West Acre.

Onwards there are no very well-defined modern path lines. Around Thetford is Breckland, where extensive deposits of glacial drift above the chalk have produced a terrain of sandy heathlands. It has been widely planted by the Forestry Commission; Thetford Forest, which covers 52,000 acres, has waymarked walks, picnic sites and an arboretum. Thetford has the largest motte in England (81ft high) and ruins of a priory and an abbey. There are several other ancient historic buildings. Here probably the Icknield Way crossed the Little Ouse.

Near Brandon, 5 miles to the north-west, are the famous Grime's Graves, one of the major objectives for travellers on the ancient trackways. Here a special stratum of flint was mined for use as shaping and cutting tools in workings covering 34 acres. Of some 300 pits operating about 2000 BC, two have been recently opened to the public, so that it is possible to see how these primitive miners lived and worked long ago.

The ancient trackways ran on towards Newmarket, possibly crossing the River Lark at Icklingham, where the O.S. Map marks 'Pilgrims' Way', possibly coinciding later with A11.

South of Newmarket is a remarkable series of linear earthworks, defensive against invaders coming from the south. The first, known as Devil's Dyke, runs for 6 miles from Burwell on the edge of the fens (protective camp nearby) to Ditton Green (camps at Cheveley and Lidgate). With an average height of 16ft above the surface, or 30ft above the parallel ditch, it was a formidable work defending the gap between the impassable fens on the one hand and impenetrable forests on the other. Seven miles or so further south is the Fleam Dyke, about four miles long, again bridging the gap between fen and forest. Two miles on we reach a Roman road, the Via Devana, which ran from Colchester to Grantchester. This extends north-westwards on to the Gog-Magog Hills, chalk heights which look down on Cambridge, named (maybe) for giant figures once carved here. On these hills too is Wandlebury Camp. The most forward of the defensive ditches is Brent Ditch by Pampisford.

South of A505 (Pampisford–Royston–Baldock) there is hilly chalk country. The county summits of Essex (458ft) and of Cambridgeshire (478ft) are only 1½ miles apart near Great Chishill. Beyond Ermine Street (now A14) the hills reach 547ft around Therfield and Kelshall. Parallel to this road on the north side is Ashwell Street, probably the line of the ancient way as it passes camps at Arbury Banks and Willbury Hill.

The Icknield Way continues parallel to the Baldock–Luton road, through Ickleford, passing close by Pirton where the isolated mound known as Toot Hill is notable. The trackway runs along the south side of the Barton Hills and reaches 602ft at Telegraph Hill; Ravensborough Camp is nearby. Finally it comes to Lea-grave; M1 is crossed and then Watling Street at Dunstable. Suddenly we reach typical chalk cuesta country, the Dunstable Downs rise up steeply, the familiar scarp facing north-west, the dip flowing south-east towards London.

Away to the north is the important camp at Totternhoe (partially destroyed by quarrying) with the auxiliary enclosure of Maiden Bower nearby. The stone for Windsor Castle came from here and there used at one time to be a mine similar to those of the North Downs.

Leaving the Icknield Way at the scarp foot, we climb to the ridge top on a minor road past Five Knolls. Soon comes the headquarters of the London Gliding Club at the foot of the scarp and sailplanes swooping and soaring can often be seen. Point 798 along this road is the county summit of Bedfordshire. Ivinghoe Beacon Hill prominent ahead, jutting out in front of the scarp, marks the start of the Ridgeway Path, while in the bay between is Whipsnade Zoo.

References
O.S. 1 inch Map Sheets 124, 125, 135, 136, 147, 148, 160

7

THE RIDGEWAY PATH

THE CHILTERN HILLS

Ivinghoe Beacon Hill–Pitstone Hill–Tring–Hastoe–Wendover
Woods–Wendover–Coombe Hill–Princes Risborough–Bledlow
Watlington–Swyncombe Downs–Nuffield–Mongewell–Goring

THE Ridgeway Path runs from Ivinghoe Beacon Hill by way of the Chiltern Hills, the Berkshire Downs and the Marlborough Downs to Overton Hill on A4 west of Marlborough. The total length is some eighty-five miles.

In the Chilterns section the Path seldom has available the straightforward obvious line of other chalk ridgeways. Clay-with-flints on the dip slopes and the ridge top and even down the scarp encourages a prolific tree cover—these hills are famous for their beech woods. Agriculture too is widespread. The route winds about therefore, sometimes on the ridge taking views where it can, sometimes at the foot of the scarp where the Upper and Lower Icknield Ways run in a situation similar to that of the Pilgrims' Way on the North Downs.

The gaps in the hills, notably those at Princes Risborough, Wendover and Tring, do not owe their origin to an original stream pattern on a dome now eroded away, as is the case for similar gaps on other chalk hills. Instead they are spill-ways cut by water trapped between here and the advancing ice-sheets of the last Ice Age. The water ran off through what were originally mere notches in the ridge, deepening them in the process into considerable channels. These gaps are utilised by the railway routes which make this part of the Chilterns into popular day walking country for Londoners. That between Tring and Berkhamsted in particular has always been an important communication channel carrying the Roman Akeman Street, the Grand Junction (now Grand Union) Canal and the main line railway from London to Birmingham and the north-west.

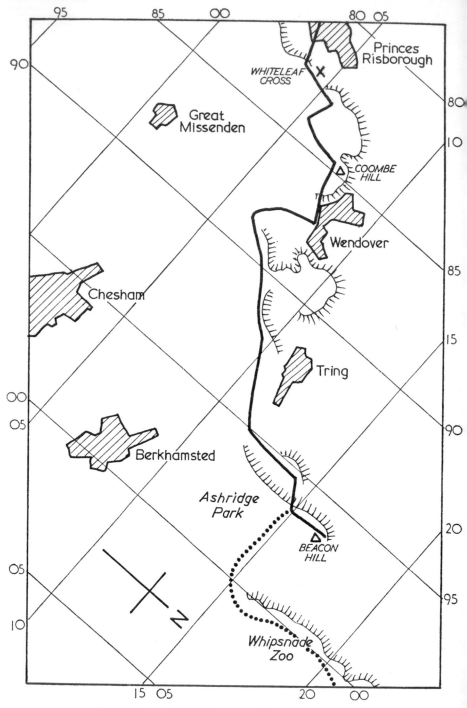

18   Ridgeway Path: Beacon Hill–Princes Risborough

It is said that there are 3,000 miles of negotiable foot and bridle paths in the Chilterns, a considerable density, so that the mere 45 miles of the Ridgeway Path only samples a minute fraction of the possibilities. Some parts are reminiscent of chalk hills elsewhere, and there is a leavening of antiquities, hill figures and so forth, but here above all one can study many aspects of trees and woodlands and their influence as a foreground or a background to hill scenery.

The following are the approximate Path distances. Ivinghoe Beacon Hill to the Grand Union Canal crossing 3½ miles, to Hastoe 3½ miles, to Wendover 4½ miles, to Princes Risborough 6½ miles, to A40 crossing 8½ miles, to Watlington 3 miles, to A4011 crossing 6 miles, to Mongewell 4½ miles, to Goring 5½ miles—a total of 45½ miles of Path.

Ivinghoe Beacon Hill with its Iron Age fort, at the tip of a north-jutting promontory, is a fine viewpoint, from which we look back eastwards along the downs over the White Lion of Whipsnade and the gliders of Dunstable. Below in the valley is Ivinghoe village (Youth Hostel, ancient church and the oldest post-mill in Britain, dating from 1627, now preserved by the National Trust). The ridge tops hereabouts are part of the 6 sq miles of the Ashridge Estate of the National Trust; this also includes five commons with walks and picnic places and the Bridgewater Monument (commemorating the English canal pioneer), where there is another good viewpoint on top of 162 steps of staircase.

We follow the ridge south to a col between Beacon Hill and Ivinghoe Hills, where there is a car park on a minor road accessible from B489. Descending Steps Hill we cross another minor road (again with car park) and climb to Pitstone Hill, an outlier of over 700ft, which looks down on the local quarries and cement works. Aldbury village lies below between here and the main scarp.

A descent now through the wood called Aldbury Nowers leads to a crossing of the railway near Tring station and further on of the Grand Union Canal a quarter of a mile west of the station.

Passing alongside Pendley Manor the route crosses Akeman Street (now A41) and comes to Tring Park. To the south is Wigginton village—a notable viewpoint. To the north:

TRING (SP91/9211). Access by A41. Main line railway station (1¾m). E.C. Wed.

See: Zoological museum. *Visit*: Nature reserves on canal reservoirs (1m N); Marsworth Locks on the Grand Union Canal (1½m N); Ashridge Estate, commons etc (3½m E); Berkhamsted Castle (5m SE); Wendover Woods (2½m SW).

From the south-west corner of Tring Park the Path passes by Hastoe village and enters the long narrow wood, running north-east to south-west, north of Point 802. This is adjacent to the road between Cholesbury and Hastoe and is the county summit of Hertfordshire. The camp at Cholesbury seems to have been on the line of part of Grim's Ditch, probably an ancient boundary, though the camp here may indicate also the existence of an ancient ridgeway.

Continuing inside the edge of the wood we come to a prominent bend in a minor road (O.S. ref SP9008) near The Crong. The line carries on south-westwards to the minor road between St Leonards and Aston Hill, on the far side of which lie Wendover Woods.

These have been developed by the Forestry Commission as an amenity centre (Wendover Forest Park). There are car parks opening off this minor road with picnic areas and five waymarked walks of various lengths, which sample many aspects of Chiltern scenery. One visits the viewpoint of Aston Hill (852ft) at the north end of the wood, another explores Beddington Banks, an earthwork in the south-west corner. Somewhere hereabouts is the county summit of Buckinghamshire, which is also the highest point of the Chiltern Hills. The highest figure given as a spot height on the O.S. Map is 857ft alongside the road, but the area

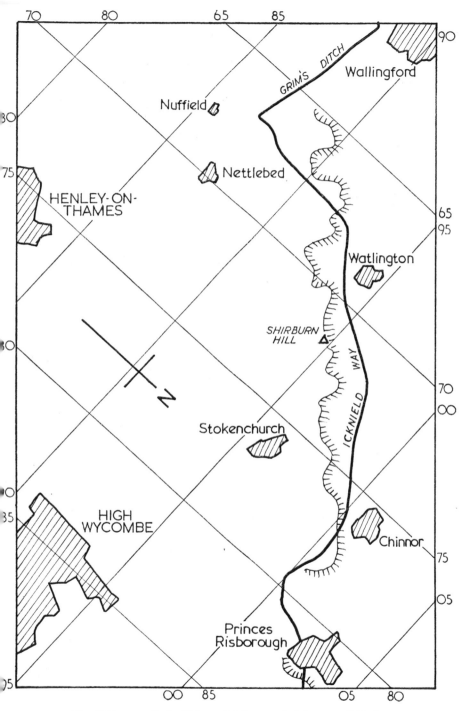

19 Ridgeway Path: Princes Risborough–Mongewell Park

of the 850ft contour ring is considerable and there may well be points higher somewhere in the woods. Forestry Commission pamphlets with detailed descriptions are readily available. The Path continues south-westerly through Hale Wood on the slopes of Cock's Hill, emerging eventually to run north-westerly to Wendover.

WENDOVER (SP86/8707/08). Access by A413 (NW and SE), A4011 (NE) and B4010 (W). Minor line railway station. Youth Hostel (2m SE). E.C. Thurs.

Another spill-way gap town. *Visit*: Wendover Forest Park (2m E); Coombe Hill (1½m WSW); Ellesborough Church (viewpoint) (2m WSW); Weston Turville Nature Reserve (1m N).

After half a mile on B4010, which here is in fact the line of the Upper Icknield Way, we strike off straight ahead up the slopes of Bacombe Hill. Soon the summit of Coombe Hill (842ft) is reached, with a monument to the South African War and a far-ranging view, which includes St Paul's Cathedral. The hill belongs to the National Trust, which in 1965 decided to clear the scrub, re-seed with appropriate grasses, fence-in and introduce sheep. The result is an expanse of grassland suitable to accommodate the many visitors. There is a Nature Trail (booklet available from the National Trust) of about one and a quarter miles.

The scarp line continues westwards to another notable viewpoint at Beacon Hill (756ft), where Cymbeline's Castle comprises two small enclosures said to be the baileys of a Norman earthwork. The Path however descends south off Coombe Hill and, by a line which has not yet been exactly determined, comes to Buckmoorend. The route continues through Chequers Park and on to the scarp face of Pulpit Hill (813ft), which has a small camp with single bank on the summit. The scarp is contoured to Long-

Page 137 Corfe Castle and the chalk ridge

Page 138 (*above*) High Stoy from Batcombe Hill, Dorset; (*below*) Badbury Rings, Dorset

down Hill, a minor road is crossed and a path followed on to White Leaf Hill. Below is the White Leaf Cross (50ft high by 25ft long with a pyramidal base 340ft wide). There is no real knowledge of its date; Massingham believed it to have been there when early man passed on his way to Grime's Graves, it may have been a waymark to Monks Risborough in medieval times, others ascribe it only to the eighteenth century. Now road and path lead us down to Princes Risborough.

PRINCES RISBOROUGH (SP8002/03/04, 8103). At the junction of A4010 and A4129. Minor line railway station. Youth Hostel (4m SSW). E.C. Wed.

Another spill-way gap town. *See*: Manor House (National Trust), seventeenth century, also other old houses. *Visit*: White Leaf Cross (1m NE); Ellesborough Church (viewpoint) (2½m NE); Bledlow Cross (2½m SW).

The Path skirts Princes Risborough on the south side using the line of the Upper Icknield Way; branching left it crosses the railway and climbs on to Lodge Hill, which is part of the Bledlow Ridge, the south-western side wall of the spill-way gap. This runs south-eastwards for 4 miles to Church Hill above West Wycombe, which is lavishly crowned by a church with a golden ball, a hill fort and a mausoleum. In addition there is a well-known show cave.

We contour Wain Hill (where the O.S. indicates a 799ft spot height yet an 800ft contour) and drop down once again to the Upper Icknield Way, here only a trackway. On this hillside is the Bledlow Cross, another of completely uncertain date and purpose.

This trackway at the foot of the scarp is followed for 8 miles. We pass below Chinnor Hill, through the quarries and cement works at Chinnor, then below Crowell Hill. At Beacon Hill comes the A40 crossing, soon to become M40 with the resulting obliteration of rural amenities; certainly the Nature Reserve

I

here can hardly survive. Once this is behind the country is quiet again. There is a parallel minor road along the ridge top, crossing Shirburn Hill (835ft) which is the county summit of Oxfordshire, and this might well be taken in places as an alternative to the Icknield Way lower down. The fortified manor-house at Shirburn village is not open to the public. Queen Wood at Christmas Common is a Forestry Commission experimental site equipped with a Nature Trail, where much can be learned about the operations of silviculture. Watlington Hill gives far-ranging views; below is the 'Mark', cut in 1764, a pyramid 16ft across the base and 90ft high.

WATLINGTON (SU6894). At the crossing of B4009 and B480. Nearest stations—Cholsey and Moulsford (10m), Princes Risborough (10m). E.C. Wed.
   See: Market Hall (1664). *Visit*: Watlington Hill (1m SE); battlefield of Chalgrove (3m NW).

Finally at a point some half a mile south-east of Britwell Salome village, the Ridgeway Path quits the Icknield Way, turning south over Swyncombe Downs, past Swyncombe House and Ewelme Park to Gongsdown Hill on A4130. It crosses Nuffield Common, passes through Nuffield village and comes to a long and well-preserved section of Grim's Ditch. Believed to have been an ancient boundary between Wessex and Mercia, this crops up in many places not only in the Chilterns but in the Berkshire Downs as well. Sometimes the bank is as much as 40ft high, the ditch up to 30ft deep. There are 3½ miles of it here, used by the Ridgeway Path, in an almost straight line to the River Thames at Mongewell.
   Through Mongewell Park, past North Stoke and South Stoke, the way runs southwards through the water meadows of the River Thames to Goring; here it is certainly no ridgeway but these flat lands contrast pleasantly with the miles of hill ridge which stretch on ahead beyond the river.

GORING (SU6080/81). Where B4526 meets B4009. Main line railway station. E.C. Wed.
   See: Norman church; River Thames. *Visit*: Checkendon church (Norman) (4m ENE).

References
O.S. 1 inch Map Sheets 159, 158
O.S. 2½ inch Map Sheets SP91, 90, 80, 70, SU79, 69, 68

STREATLEY TO THE MARLBOROUGH DOWNS

Streatley–Blewbury Down (East and West Ilsley)–Scutchamer Knob–Segsbury Camp (Letcombe Bassett)–Devil's Punchbowl (Lambourn and Lambourn Downs)–Uffington White Horse (Bishopstone)–Liddington Castle

Ahead now the Berkshire Downs offer nearly thirty miles of well-defined north facing scarp with trackways most of the way and only the occasional road crossing, until finally we come to Wiltshire and M4. Unlike the Chilterns this is the typical bare hill country of the chalk, a real introduction to the vast expanses of the same rock found further west. The scarp marks the edge of the chalk block which widens to the south as we come nearer to Wiltshire and the Marlborough Downs, so that beyond Wantage there are several miles of chalk downland on the dip slope stretching down to Lambourn and beyond, famous racehorse country. To the north is the Vale of the White Horse, in fact the valley of the River Ock which flows to join the Thames at Abingdon. The Thames itself after a huge bend at Oxford turns finally west and runs parallel to the Ock further north beyond the Corallian Ridge.

'A spreading view of middle England', wrote Hippisley Cox in

1934, 'stretches away to the north, with the Thames in the near distance, and it is said that on clear days the smoke of Birmingham can be seen, more than a hundred miles away.'

From Streatley to the A34 crossing is 6½ miles; between A34 and A338 is another 6½ miles; from A338 crossing to Uffington White Horse is also 6½ miles and finally another 7½ miles bring us to M4 crossing and Liddington Castle—a total of 27 miles. We cross the Thames by Goring Lock over to:

STREATLEY (SU58/5980). Access by A329 from Reading and Wallingford, A417 from Wantage, B4526 from the east and B4009 from the west. Nearest station—Streatley and Goring (at Goring ¾m). Youth Hostel. E.C. Thurs.

See: Lardon Chase and Lough Down, National Trust holdings on the hills immediately above with fine views; the Thames.

The Ridgeway Path follows A417 for half a mile round the slopes of Lough Down, then turns westwards on a trackway running up into the hills in a valley between here and Thurle Down. In just over three miles a cross track is reached with Lowbury Hill (611ft) a spur on the right. On the left a route involving only a small amount of road walking can be followed past Perborough Castle (SU5278) and Grimsbury Castle (SU5172) earthworks almost to Newbury.

Alternative routes for this first section join in hereabouts. A possible alternative line of the Great Ridgeway followed B4009 out of Streatley for 2½ miles to Hungerford Green, where a left turn leads to a trackway to Starveall and so to this point by Lowbury Hill. If, instead of following the Thames on the Ridgeway Route from South Stoke, we had been able to cross the river to Moulsford (unfortunately there is no bridge), a footpath could have been taken to A417 followed by the trackway called 'The Fair Mile' over Cholsey Downs to Lowbury Hill. The north-

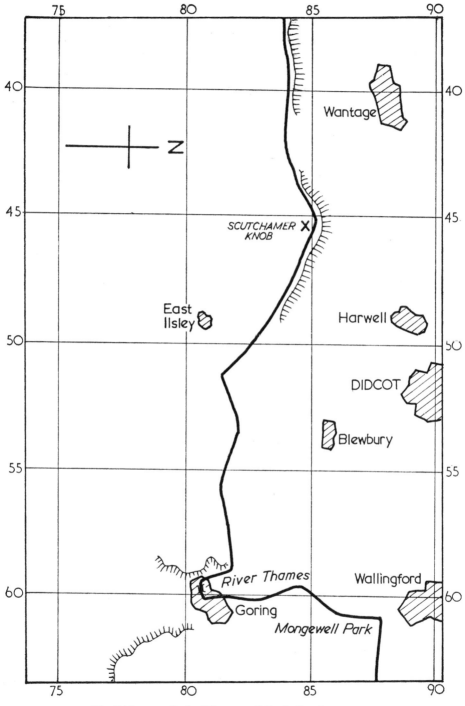

20   Ridgeway Path: Mongewell Park–Segsbury Camp

bound trackway on Lowbury Hill is called the 'White Hollow Way' and leads down to A417 near Aston Tirrold, where there is a fort on Blewburton Hill. Nearby is

BLEWBURY (SU5385). On A417. Access also by B4016 from Didcot. Nearest station—Didcot (4m). E.C. Thurs.
See: Church, half-timbered houses.

Back on the Ridgeway Route we come in half a mile to Roden Down where there is a complex meeting place of trackways from all points of the compass. We continue straight ahead for another half mile, then fork left and cross the old Didcot–Newbury railway on Blewbury Down. There are several alternative routes, but the dead straight line of the original Great Ridgeway seems no longer permissible. The official route descends over Compton Down, then turns right along Several Down to Gore Hill on A34. A mile and a half south, just off A34, is:

EAST ILSLEY (SU4980/81). Access from A34. Nearest station— Didcot (9m), Newbury (9m). E.C. Wed. A horse-racing village.

The Ridgeway Route now runs absolutely straight for 2 miles over Bury Down, passing a minor road access point, to a meeting place of trackways on East Hendred Down (612ft). The left-hand track can be followed towards Newbury in the south, with only a quarter of a mile of road, until cut off by the scars of M4. At this point on the downs there is little incentive to look out over the Vale of the White Horse, where the Atomic Energy Research Station at Harwell gives us another reminder of the curious material philosophies on which our civilisation is based. The feeling that the best has already passed is inescapable.

A little over half a mile ahead is a very large tumulus, once 77ft

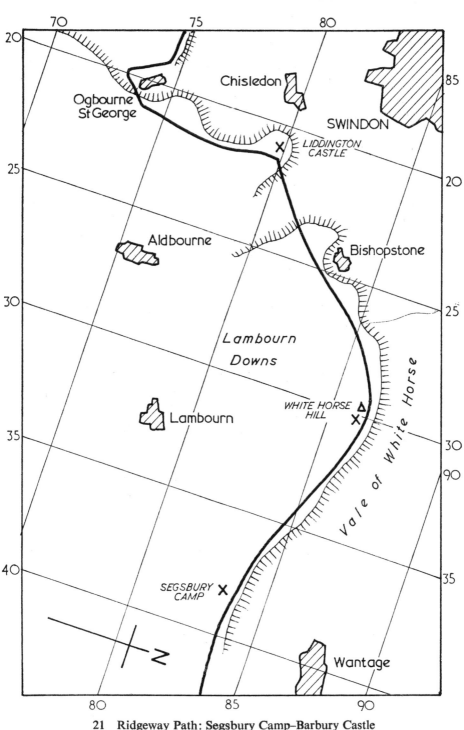

21 Ridgeway Path: Segsbury Camp–Barbury Castle

high and 400ft round the base but much reduced by misguided archaeological excavation, now known as Scutchamer Knob. Hippisley Cox called it Cwichelmes Low, while Timperley and Brill found that it has been called at various times Scutchamfly Barrow and Scotchman's Hob. Its beech trees were once a landmark; these have been felled but newly planted trees (1965) promise to restore the distinction as the years go on. It is Saxon, probably seventh century; certainly it is mentioned in the Saxon Chronicles for AD 1000—'The Danes after destroying Walling-ford passed the night at Cholsey, and then turned along Ashdown at Cwichelmes Low.' It is a mile and a half now over Ridgeway Down to Betterton Down and a white monument to Baron Wantage, which Hippisley Cox terms 'offensively conspicuous'. B4494 is soon crossed and we continue over Lattin Down, turn left past Whitehouse Farm and come to A338. Two and a half miles north is

WANTAGE (SU39/4087/88). Access by A417 from east and west, A338 from north and south. Nearest station—Didcot (9m). E.C. Thurs.

The birthplace of King Alfred (AD 849), his statue is in the market place. *See*: Church; Bear Inn. *Visit*: Uffington Castle earthwork and the White Horse (6½m W); Segsbury Camp (2½m SSW); Letcombe Bassett; the Devil's Punchbowl (3½m SW).

Three quarters of a mile beyond A338 is Segsbury Camp (or Letcombe Castle), which stands on the 700ft contour on Castle Hill to the right of the track. It is 27 acres but the defences are not formidable. The Ridgeway Path sweeps round a large embayment in the scarp with Letcombe Bassett village at the foot. After Folly Clump and Green Down (762ft) we reach B4001 which runs down a spur called Hackpen Hill towards Wantage. Between here and the scarp on the east side is the tremendous combe of the Devil's Punchbowl. In this section there are several trackways off southwards which can be followed as far as the valley of the Lambourn. Four and a half miles south is

LAMBOURN (SU3278/79). Access by B4001. Nearest station— Hungerford (9m). E.C. Thurs.

Another important horse-racing centre. *See*: Church; ancient cross.

The route continues north-westerly over Point 793 and Point 747 to a minor road crossing above Blowingstone Hill. 'A little way down the Kingston Lisle road,' writes Hippisley Cox, 'in a cottage garden on the right, is the celebrated Blowing Stone, brought here from the Ridgeway nearly fifty years ago. Those who know the trick can, by blowing into a hollow produce a sound like that of a foghorn and it is seldom that one of the beautiful girls from the cottage is unwilling to instruct the stranger.'

We have now reached one of the outstanding sites of south country chalk—the Uffington White Horse. It is a stylised figure, 365ft long and 130ft high, dating from the first or second century BC. The original significance is lost to us though the outline is similar to those on Belgic coinage of the period. It is of course considerably older and quite different from all the others. Below the head is a deep combe called the Manger; above on the ridge top is Uffington Castle, an 8 acre earthwork with formidable bank and ditch; there is also a car park. The eastern side of the Manger is formed by Dragon, or Pendragon Hill, where St George slew the dragon.

These hill figures need regular weeding and cleaning to maintain the outline and this process was at one time made the excuse for a local holiday with a fair and games in and around Uffington Castle. We are fortunate that the last of these, held in 1857, was carefully described by Tom Hughes, better known perhaps for

Tom Brown's Schooldays, in his *The Scouring of the White Horse,* a book which really tells us what the countryside is about seen through the eyes of a townsman: 'The turf was as soft as a feather bed, and as springy as horsehair; and it was all covered with thistledown, which came drifting along like snow with the south wind; all down below the country looked so rich and peaceful, stretching out for miles at my feet in the hazy sunshine, and the larks right up overhead sang so sweetly, that I didn't know whether to laugh or cry.'

A mile ahead a copse of beeches beside the trackway conceals Wayland Smith's Cave, the remains of a megalithic tomb, which is mentioned in Sir Walter Scott's *Kenilworth.* Between here and Uffington Castle a number of trackways and paths strike off southwards across the Lambourn Downs. The casual walker will always have to stop short of M4 motorway which bars the way to the Kennet and the Inkpen Ridgeway, but the country as far as the River Lambourn will still be relatively pleasant. There are racehorse training facilities and antiquarian remains, notably Seven Barrows (SU3282). The number quoted is curious for there are in fact many more. Seven seems to have had some magical quality for there are other sites similarly named which are similarly overendowed.

We press on with the Ridgeway Path which now runs south-westerly over a broad down towards Charlbury Hill (829ft). Off to the left is the four-storey Ashdown House (National Trust), which is built of chalk blocks and is surmounted by a cupola with a golden ball. In the grounds is the small Iron Age fort of Alfred's Castle. We cross presently into Wiltshire. On the scarp slopes above Bishopstone are found some of the finest examples of strip lynchets in the chalk country. For cultivation purposes the hillside was divided into horizontal strips separated by low banks, thus forming a series of steps. These date from medieval times.

Hippisley Cox could write that the view beyond Wanborough Plain of 'Liddington Castle with the sun setting behind it is magnificent, the frowning outline of the hill resembling an immense fortress dominating all the land.' Now, however, M4 motorway has taken care of all that. We cross it and come to the Marlborough Downs.

References
O.S. 1 inch Map Sheets 157, 158
O.S. $2\frac{1}{2}$ inch Map Sheets SU58, 48, 38, 28, 27

Appendices

I

CHALK

CHALK is a relatively soft and friable form of limestone (almost pure calcium carbonate), composed of fossil sea shells, some so small that they can only be seen under a microscope, bedded in a fine-grained matrix of shell remains. It was formed beneath the sea in the Cretaceous period between 60 and 120 million years ago, when dinosaurs and other large monsters were roaming the adjacent land. In these same Cretaceous seas there were also life-forms with siliceous shells or support frames, which contributed small quantities of silica to the sea-bed rock. Subsequently, after geological forces had elevated the chalk from the seas, percolating surface waters began to dissolve the silica, redepositing it in the form of completely insoluble flint nodules each a mosaic of very small quartz crystals. These flint masses, often grotesquely shaped, are usually scattered in layers parallel to the bedding planes, though they sometimes occur also in the form of sheets or in vertical veins along joint planes. Similar aggregations of siliceous materials, found in other limestones or indeed in other rock formations, are known generally as chert, of which flint might be regarded as a special form. Chert sometimes takes the form of bedded layers several feet thick which can, as we shall see, modify land forms because of its resistance to erosion. The essentially nodular flint, on the other hand, is left behind when chalk is eroded away forming flint gravels in river valleys, the notable clay-with-flints soil which sometimes caps the chalk hills, or flint beaches along the sea coast.

The deposition of chalk ended with the rise of the sea floor and there was dry land of gentle relief over much of south-east England, being slowly denuded by streams flowing across it to the surrounding seas. It was only by the Miocene of the Tertiary period (some 25 million years ago) that present-day relief at last began to take shape. The effects of the great uplift processes which produced the Alpine ranges of Europe, though considerably diminished, were still felt this far away. The chalk with the clays and sands beneath was pushed up into a series of domes or ridges, the largest of which covered most of present-day south-east England and extended beyond where the English Channel now is, into northern France. The break-through of the waters to form the Channel took place only recently—about 5000 BC. There was another dome, much smaller, above the present Vale of Pewsey and yet another in the southern part of the Isle of Wight. The present extensive chalk exposure in the counties of Hampshire and Wiltshire was an area of general uplift, covered at the time by a layer of sandstone, and lacked the dome or ridge pattern of the others.

A new drainage pattern developed as streams flowed down the sides of the domes, while various agents of erosion went to work on the higher parts. The centre was gradually lowered; the whole of the chalk cover eventually disappeared exposing older rocks, such as Upper and Lower Greensand, in the centre, leaving a rim of chalk facing steeply inwards where the immediately underlying and readily eroded strata thus exposed were more rapidly worn away. The steep inward slopes are known as the scarp and the gentle outer slopes as the dip—the whole geological entity is called a cuesta. The relative steepness of scarp and dip depends on the dip of the strata; if the angle of dip is sufficiently high both sides of the cuesta may have comparable angles, if low the angles are noticeably different. As the planing-off continued the stream pattern radiating from the original summit was still maintained by down-cutting, which continued to operate on the hills of the rim as the centre of the area continued to depress. This explains the apparent anomaly in the present-day scene of streams which flow from the Weald north and south towards the chalk hills and breach them by deep river gaps. The curious drainage pattern in the Vale of Pewsey and in the Isle of Wight can be explained in the same way. Similarly the break-through of the River Thames from the north of the chalk hills into the London Basin was initiated at a time when the ground level to

Page 155 (*above*) The cliffs at Bempton, East Riding; (*below*) Dunstable Downs, looking across to Ivinghoe

Page 156   The summit of Coombe Hill, Chilterns

the north was higher than that of the chalk hills. The real marvel of these various phenomena lies not in the dimensions of the river gaps, though these indeed appear large compared with the sizes of the streams, but in the tremendous amount of material which must have been removed from the higher reaches.

Meanwhile the down-folds in the chalk strata were covered with new deposits—sands, clays and gravels—notably in the London Basin, the lower valley of the River Thames, where the chalk dips far below the present surface, and the Hampshire Basin, which was partially flooded subsequently by an extensive breakdown of the southern chalk rim by the sea.

The surface exposure of the chalk, as we see it today, has a very distinctive pattern. In the counties of Wiltshire, western Berkshire and northern Hampshire a central block of high chalk country forms Salisbury Plain and the Marlborough Downs. This sometimes presents outward-facing steep scarps such as those around the north-west corner of the Marlborough Downs, along the north-eastern edge above the Kennet Valley, in the complex of river valleys west of Salisbury, and so on. In the west the Vale of Pewsey marks the site of a small eroded dome, with scarps on the north and south—a miniature Weald. The main drainage (the River Avon) is not, as might be expected, from east to west, but breaks through the south wall towards Salisbury.

From this central block there radiates a series of chalk ridges. The longest, starting in the north-east corner, runs eastwards as the Berkshire Downs to the point where the River Thames breaks through at the Goring Gap then continues north-eastwards as the Chiltern Hills. However, the gaps in these hills were not made by down-cutting of streams but were spillways for water trapped between here and ice advancing from the north. Beyond Dunstable the chalk spreads out and loses its cuesta character; though there are extensive recent glacial deposits, the outcrops can nevertheless be followed and there is often typical chalk country scenery through East Anglia to the sea coast cliffs near Hunstanton and elsewhere. On the far side of the Wash are the

K

low chalk ridges of the Lincolnshire Wolds, which culminate beyond the Humber in the magnificent Yorkshire Wolds and great sea-cliffs at Bempton and Flamborough Head. The second chalk ridge continues the line of the Newbury Downs, the highest chalk hills in England, and, after a depression between Basingstoke and Farnham, rises along the Hog's Back to the North Downs, the rim of the great Wealden Dome. These hills present a south-facing scarp for more than a hundred miles until cut-off by the sea at Dover. There are prominent river gaps cut by the Rivers Wey, Mole, Darent, Medway and Stour. The third ridge runs east from the central block in Hampshire and on entering Sussex, takes on great individual character as the South Downs. The scarp faces north across the Weald. This ridge, broken by gaps cut by the rivers Arun, Adur, and Cuckmere, is truncated by the sea near Eastbourne.

In its south-western corner the centre block is broken up by some minor river valleys to give the short ridges traversed by the Grovely Ridgeway, the Salisbury Way and the Ox Drove Way. The main line of the ridge runs south-westwards with a scarp above Blackmoor Vale and a long dip slope to the south and east which is Cranborne Chase. The River Stour flows through a gap by Blandford Forum, then the great chalk ridge flows on with north facing scarp as far as Toller Down Gate in Dorset. Continuing westwards, the chalk only occurs in isolated patches; it does, however, end in a truly magnificent sea-cliff at Beer Head in East Devon.

From Toller Down Gate the main chalk outcrop, losing for a time its cuesta character, passes south towards Eggardon Hill and then runs back eastwards between Dorchester and the sea, to reach the coast at White Nothe and Swyre Head by Durdle Door. Further east the limestone has protected the chalk ridge which runs parallel to the sea's edge, but now is a short distance inland. This ridge is an upstanding feature of the inland countryside all along the Purbeck Hills to the sea at the Foreland by Swanage. Fifteen miles away the chalk cliffs of the Needles and Scratchell's Bay in the Isle of Wight are the continuation of the ridge, the intervening section of which has been removed by the sea since it first broke through into the Hampshire Basin. On the Island the chalk ridge runs from west to east across the centre to finish at Culver Cliffs near Bembridge. There is a further short ridge in the south running from St Catherine's Point to Shanklin; between the two ridges the rock pattern provides an eroded Wealden dome in miniature.

The outstanding characteristics of chalk country are the green rounded hillsides, with no natural exposure of rock anywhere inland, the considerable extent of the cuesta land-forms, their outline dependent on the dip of the strata, the lack of surface drainage, the light-coloured soils full of fantastic-shaped flint nodules and the remains everywhere of early man. The Wolds have been widely developed agriculturally and cultivation sweeps all over the tops; on Salisbury Plain, on the other hand, the dead hand of military occupation has meant desolation, destruction and enclosures, and activity is ceaseless.

The great chalk ridges, with their varying scarps and dips, are sometimes very impressive in outline, particularly where valleys draining the dip slope have cut back until their heads almost reach the scarp edge, so that the summit traveller has big distant views on either hand. Often, too, they look steep and wall-like from the scarp foot plains. Gilbert White called the South Downs 'a chain of majestic mountains'; a modern view would regard them rather as essentially fulfilling what we mean by 'hills' as distinct from mountains, which should be harsh, rugged and less flowing in line. Nowhere are the chalk hills too steep to hold vegetation.

The soil cover however is certainly thin and this has encouraged the art of the famous chalk hill-figures. Man has exposed the rock in two other ways—the first by quarrying, the vast white scars of which are visible for many a mile, the second by ploughing, where light-coloured soil and the profusion of flints combine to provide a unique tillage. Only at the sea coast is natural chalk exposed by the under-cutting action of the sea. The gently inclined beds are removed and the upper part of the cliff collapses to the beach, leaving behind walls which are often vertical and sometimes even overhanging. A little rock climbing has been done, but unfortunately English chalk, apart perhaps from the untried cliffs at Bempton in Yorkshire, seems considerably softer than the French, which outcrops along the Seine Valley in walls and pinnacles which seem to have resisted erosion to an extent not matched on this side of the Channel. In many seacliffs the horizontal arrangement of the flint layers is a distinctive feature, while the beaches below are composed almost entirely of flint nodules.

The porosity of the chalk is the main reason why such comparatively soft material should form upstanding hill ridges at all: it is just not eroded, as are a good many materials far harder, by the flow of surface water. When rock strata are permeable there is no surface drainage as long as the water-table is below the surface. So called 'dry valleys' which look as though they were once carved by water but have no present streams, were formed either when the ground was impermeable due to freezing or when the water-table was higher than it is today. Indeed fluctuations in the water-table produce conditions of intermittent flow in some chalk valleys. As with Mountain Limestone, one would expect to find cave formation taking place due to water solution and small natural caves have in fact been discovered in the chalk—notably, in this country, at Strood near Rochester. However, the rock is not sufficiently massive to sustain the considerable stream passages and chambers which are found in harder limestones, nor indeed are the chalk hills high enough to produce the necessary volumes of water. Man-made holes and tunnels, constructed for a wide variety of uses, have been located in various places, but many are in a dangerous state and they are progressively being blocked off.

Where permeable chalk is folded into a syncline with impermeable beds above and below, as in the London Basin, the chalk strata become a huge reservoir for water which enters at the edges and permeates to the centre. Wells bored in the basin down to the chalk tap water which is at sufficient pressure to rise to the surface and this was what used to happen with Artesian wells of

London. However, excessive removal of water has so reduced the level that water can now only be raised by pumping.

Chalk streams sometimes run below ground, the outstanding example being the River Mole in the Dorking Gap, which at times when the flow is not excessive sinks into swallow holes by Mickleham to reappear some way further on. It is unlikely that the stream passages through which it flows are large enough for cavers to enter the system, though there are the usual stories of penetration by ducks and others.

The characteristic vegetation cover of the chalk hills is the famous springy turf, though it is said that this results from extensive use as pasturage and that woodlands would grow again if the sheep were removed. Early man may have found dense woods of beech and pine, the remains of which may still appear as small clumps of woodland on the upper slopes. But a superficial cover of other material can result in a very different vegetation, typically when there is a deposit of clay-with-flints, a residual soil made up of the debris left after the complete removal of large masses of chalk. Then, as on the North Downs, the Chiltern Hills or in Savernake Forest, we find woodlands growing up and over the high crests. Many of the downland beech woods, such as that crowning Chanctonbury Ring, are of comparatively recent date.

In many places in the chalk country, but notably in the Marlborough Downs area of Wiltshire, the one-time over-lying strata included a layer of hard sandstone with the grains bound together by silica. Large blocks of this left deposited on the present-day chalk surface are called sarsens, grey wethers, Druid stones or bridestones. Early man, already attracted to chalk areas by their dryness and by the abundance of workable flints, used the larger sarsens for the construction of the great stone circles such as those at Avebury and Stonehenge. (See Appendix II.)

Bibliography
Davies, G. M. *The Geology of London and South East England,* 1939
Shepherd, W. *Flint: Its Origins, Properties and Uses,* 1973
Topley, W. *The Geology of the Weald,* 1875
Trueman, A. E. *Geology and Scenery in England and Wales,* 1949

II

THE ARCHAEOLOGY OF THE CHALK

THE prehistoric and early historic periods in the story of Britain
are divided on a basis of the progressive improvement in the
materials used for tools, and later of the methods and customs—
the general way of life—of invading peoples coming from the
continent. Until 5000 BC Great Britain was joined to the con-
tinental land mass by a land bridge on the site of the present
Straits of Dover, so the interchange of wandering humans, of
animals and of flora was readily possible. After that date the only
influences which could be brought to bear had first to cross the
sea. Table 1 summarises these archaeological periods:

TABLE 1

Dates	Name of Period	Remarks
2M–100K BC	Lower and Middle Palaeolithic ⎫ Stone	Man was a hunter and a nomad using primitive
100K–12K BC	Upper Palaeolithic ⎰ Age	flint implements. Only
12K–3K BC	Mesolithic ⎭	fragmentary remains
3K–1·8K BC	Neolithic (Stone in Britain—bronze in use elsewhere)	Farming and settled living introduced (cause-wayed camps, flint mines, megalithic tombs, long barrows, simple henges)
1·8K–550 BC	Bronze Age (following invasion by the 'Beaker Folk')	Development of an advanced civilisation in Wessex (henges fully developed, trackways widely used, round barrows)
550 BC–AD 43	Iron Age	Hill forts, dew ponds

Dates	Name of Period	Remarks
AD 43–410	Roman Britain	Characteristic forts, roads, and villas
AD 410–1066	The Dark Ages	Invasions by Saxons, Vikings and Danes (linear earthworks)
1066–1500	The Middle Ages (Medieval Britain)	Mottes, castle and cathedral building, roads
1500 to date	The Modern Age	Modern forts, canals, railways, most hill figures, chalk and hearthstone mines, windmills, general industrial remains

The principal archaeological items likely to be found in chalk country are listed below:

Barrows, long These were burial mounds used by Neolithic peoples—100 to 300ft long by 30 to 100ft wide and 4 to 12ft high. About 200 survive; the best areas are the Marlborough Downs, around Stonehenge, Cranborne Chase and the hills to the south-west, between Dorchester and Bridport and along the South Downs.

Barrows, round These were the tombs of the Bronze Age. More than 10,000 exist (4,000 in Wessex) divided according to shape and structure among Bowl, Bell, Disc and Ring Barrows, all with or without ditches. Silbury Hill (125ft) by Avebury may be a large burial or memorial mound, the exact purpose is not known.

Causewayed camps This is the name given to large non-military enclosures consisting of a single bank, with an external ditch crossed at intervals by causeways. These were used in the Neolithic period for keeping cattle or trading, and there were dwellings built against the inner side of the bank. There are good examples at Windmill Hill on the Marlborough Downs, at Knap Hill and the Trundle.

Cursus   These are long parallel banks with outside ditches, having a purpose which is still unclear to us. That at Stonehenge is 3,000yd long and 100yd wide. The Dorset Cursus on Cranborne Chase has a length of 6¼ miles.

Dew ponds   Some of these may date to the Iron Age. They are dug in the chalk, lined with impervious layers of puddled clay and straw, filled by rain and by condensation from the atmosphere.

Earthworks, linear   Some are boundaries, with the bank some-times on one side of the ditch sometimes on the other, some defensive, with the bank always upslope from the ditch. Bokerley Dyke in Cranborne Chase served both purposes; the Wansdyke along the hills above the Vale of Pewsey was defensive, a protec-tion against the Saxons. Fleam Dyke and Devil's Dyke in Cambridgeshire bar the Icknield way. These are major examples, there are many lesser.

Forts, hill   These mostly date from the Iron Age and were con-structed to overawe the earlier inhabitants or as inter-tribal strongholds. There are many fine examples in the chalk country— the story of their development is complex and worthy of study in detail elsewhere. Outstanding are Maiden Castle, Badbury Rings, Yarnbury, Cissbury, the Trundle, Old Sarum, etc. Many, such as Maiden Castle and Hod Hill, were held against the Romans and stormed in the course of the fighting.

Forts, modern   Castles were built for coastal defence during the reign of Henry VIII, eg at Walmer and Deal. The Martello Towers of the South Coast date to the Napoleonic Wars. There are coastal defences from the last century around Portsmouth and Dover. Along the North Downs various forts were planned during the late 1880s for the defence of London. Only the storehouse build-ings were actually constructed and some remain eg on Betsom's

Hill (where the 2½ inch O.S. Map marks the summit as 'Fort Westerham, disused') and above Betchworth chalk pit.

Forts, Roman   These are seldom found among chalk hills, though there is one built in the corner of the older earthwork on Hod Hill. Staging camps are found on some Roman roads, such as Stane Street. Their coastal defence forts remain as substantial ruins at Pevensey, Richborough, Reculver etc.

Henges   Henges are ceremonial structures consisting of circles of stones or wood; they probably also had an astronomical significance (see Stonehenge p 17). They date from the Neolithic period originally with later improvements. Avebury and Stonehenge are unsurpassed, but there are others worthy.

Hill figures   This is a general name for designs cut in the hillside turf, exposing the underlying rock—usually chalk—and thus conspicuous for many miles. The really ancient ones are the White Horse of Uffington (a stylised horse of the first or second century BC), the Cerne Abbas Giant (Celtic or second century) and the Long Man of Wilmington (Celtic or Saxon). There are other horses at Westbury (1778); Cherhill (1780); Pewsey (1785); Marlborough, on Granham Hill (1804); Alton Barnes (1812); Hackpen Hill (1838); Broadtown Down (1863); and Pewsey II (1937) in the central chalk area; also further afield at Sutton Poyntz, Dorset (1815) and Litlington, Cambridgeshire (1838). The Chilterns show two crosses, at Whiteleaf and Bledlow, and the Watlington 'Mark', as well as the modern lion of Whipsnade. Sundry emblems with military connections are to be found around Salisbury Plain.

Medieval castles   Castle building began around the time of the Conquest. The first castles, of the so-called motte-and-bailey type, were earth structures consisting of a mound and an enclosure, usually side by side with wooden pallisades around. Stone work was added subsequently giving the type known as a shell keep. The development of the keep as a strong point led to the construction of square, round and multi-sided towers inside some sort of curtain wall. Later came the concentric castle, imported by the Crusaders, a series of complete wall circles built one inside the other. As times became more settled more comfort was gradually provided in the shape of larger windows and so on, leading eventually to the fortified manor house. The age of castles ended abruptly with Cromwell for they were no match for gunpowder. The chalk lands of south-east England are not a good area for a comprehensive castle study, but Rochester, Arundel, Dover and Castle Rising are among those which should not be missed.

Mines, chalk Chalk for use on the land was obtained in some areas by boring through overlying strata (see notes on dene-holes p 47) and in others by tunnelling, as at Chislehurst (eighteenth century). The remains of these workings can still be entered in some places and provide a highly dangerous and not recommendable caving experience for the keen enthusiast. The few places which are maintained as show caves such as Chislehurst, Reigate etc are of course exceptions.

Mines, flint The demand by Neolithic farmers for flints for use as implements could not be met by surface collection and shafts were dug to flint-bearing seams below ground. The major sites were at Grime's Graves near Brandon in Norfolk (where open shafts may still be inspected) and on Cissbury, Blackpatch, Findon and Harrow Hills in Sussex.

Mines, hearthstone This rock was reached by tunnelling into the Upper Greensand at the base of the chalk, notably in the North Downs, at Betchworth, Godstone, Merstham, Gatton and Reigate. The material was used as a building stone and later as a floor for hearths and furnaces (see p 59). A similar building rock was obtained at and below the surface at Totternhoe in the Chilterns.

Mottes The huge earth mound which formed the strong point of the earliest type of Norman castle; see, for example, at Lewes, Farnham, Thetford etc.

Roads, medieval The present road system grew piecemeal from a local network linking villages and manors, hence its zigzag and winding nature. The development of the road network provides a fascinating study (see, for example, Cochrane, C. *The Lost Roads of Wessex*).

Roads, prehistoric Most of the routes described in this book follow very ancient trackways along the scarp edge, or at the foot of the steepest part of the scarp face, of the chalk ridges of south-east England. They came into being as Neolithic settlements demanded routes for communication and trade, reaching full development in the Iron Age. Some were later utilised by the Romans.

Roads, Roman These mostly cross the chalk ridges in their straight line journeys from point to point over the countryside. Ancient lines were used if they happened to run in the right direction, but by now the centre of the country was no longer Salisbury Plain.

Tombs, megalithic These are very similar to long barrows, but incorporate a stone burial chamber. They are mostly found in the highland parts of the country, but there are a few in the chalk area, notably West Kennett near Avebury, Wayland Smith's Cave near the Uffington White Horse and a group in Kent including Kit's Coty House and those at Addington.

Villas, Roman As soon as Britain settled peacefully after the Roman invasion, richer members of the community built country villas (600 are known, 75 of them luxury). No very extensive examples remain, but as good as any are those at Bignor, Brading and Titsey.

Windmills Built to supply motive power for various uses, notably for the grinding of corn. The oldest existing mills date to the seventeenth century. Numbers began to diminish in the nineteenth century; now over 1,500 are derelict, less than 100 are in working order. Two types can be distinguished—post mills where the whole structure rotates so that the sails face into the wind, and smock mills, where the top capping alone rotates on a fixed tower.

Bibliography
Allcroft, A. H. *Earthworks of England,* 1908
Ashbee, P. *The Bronze Age round Barrow in Britain,* 1960
Atkinson, R. J. C. *Stonehenge,* 1960
——. *Stonehenge, Avebury and Neighbouring Monuments,* 1959
Braun, H. *The English Castle,* 1936, 1942
Clarke, R. Rainbird. *East Anglia,* 1960
Cochrane, C. *The Lost Roads of Wessex,* Newton Abbot, 1969
Copley, G. J. *An Archaeology of South East England,* 1958
Cottrell, L. *Seeing Roman Britain,* 1956
Cox, R. Hippisley. *The Green Roads of England,* 1934
Crawford, O. G. S. *Wessex from the Air,* 1928
Curwen, E. C. *The Archaeology of Sussex,* 1954
Grinsell, L. V. *The Ancient Burial Mounds of England,* 1953
——. *The Archaeology of Wessex,* 1958
Hawkes, J. *Guide to Prehistoric and Roman Monuments in England and Wales,* 1951
Henderson, J., Hillman, B. and Pearman, H. *More Secret Tunnels in Surrey,* 1968
Jessup, R. F. *The Archaeology of Kent,* 1930
——. *South East England,* 1970
Marples, M. *White Horses and Other Hill Figures,* 1949
Peake, H. J. *The Archaeology of Berkshire,* 1931
Pearman, H. *Dene Holes,* 1966
——. *Secret Tunnels in Surrey,* 1963
Skilton, C. P. *British Windmills and Watermills,* 1947
Stone, J. F. S. *Wessex before the Celts,* 1958
Thomas, N. *Guide to Prehistoric England,* 1961
Timperley, H. W. and Brill, E. *Ancient Trackways of Wessex,* 1965
Whimster, D. *The Archaeology of Surrey,* 1931
Wood, E. S. *Collins Field Guide to Archaeology,* 1963

III

BIRDS OF THE CHALK

by Cyril Manning

THE object of this appendix is to be of some practical help and guidance to the walker traversing the counties covered by this book. No doubt the more experienced ornithologist and bird-watcher will already be in possession of the necessary bird identification pocket book. Many such books have been published of recent years, and take up very little space in one's haversack. The general idea here is to give brief descriptions of the various birds and their habitat. To avoid undue repetition, we will group them into families.

Crows are the most widely distributed birds in the world. The largest is the Raven. It is less abundant than its relatives, being distinguished from them by a voice which is deeper, and more resonate. The bill is massive, and in flight the outer wing feathers are spread somewhat like the extended fingers of a hand. The nest is usually placed high in a very tall tree, or quarry face, preferably under an overhang. It is our earliest breeder, often having eggs before the end of February.

Carrion Crows are very common everywhere, and are usually seen singly or in pairs. Like the Raven they are completely black, but are several inches smaller, with a more raucous voice. In flight the square tail is sufficient to distinguish it from the larger bird. What a familiar sight it is to see and hear the bustle and activity in a large rookery. The nests are placed high in the tree, often elms being chosen, and very early in the year the Rooks start repairing the old nests, or build new. It has a quicker flight than the Crow, is gregarious and identified by its whitish-grey bill.

Jackdaws also are sociable birds, and will often associate in large flocks with Rooks, a sight that is often witnessed at dusk. The sure means of identification is the grey head, and bright bead-like eyes, otherwise it is all black. The Magpie is a member of the Crow family needing no description. It cannot be mistaken for any other bird. An old country superstition regarding the Magpies is as follows: 'One for sorrow, two for joy, three for a wedding, four for a boy.' It builds a very elaborate nest situated often in a thorn tree. One of the sentinels of the countryside is the colourful Jay; its loud alarm call can be quite startling. It is vividly marked with bright blue and black barred wing feathers, light red-brown breast, and a white rump, which is very noticeable as it flies away.

Many of our common birds are found in greater numbers on the fringes of towns and villages than they are in the more open country of the downs. Food supplies could have a bearing on this. We are becoming a nation of bird lovers as the various bird tables and nesting boxes will testify, but this does not mean, however, that we shall not see the more common birds on our walk. I expect most of us at some time will have noticed those tremendous flocks of birds almost resembling a cloud, as thousands of Starlings whirl and twist before perhaps settling into a seed bed, or a stubble field. Wood-pigeons also, especially in autumn and winter, may be seen in enormous flocks, much to the chagrin of the farmer.

Blackbirds and Thrushes are so much part of the country scene that we fail to appreciate them, and yet in early summer their respective songs give us a wonderful melody. The Missel Thrush, the largest resident thrush, is also known as the 'Storm Cock', as it has a habit of perching on the topmost branches of tall trees and facing into the wind. Over the higher downs during early spring the Ring Ousel appears. It is a bird of mountain and rocky moorland. At first glimpse it resembles a Blackbird, but may be distinguished by a deep white crescent on the breast, and a harsh alarm note. From October, all through the winter months until March or April, the walker will see two other species of Thrush, which breed in the far north, and migrate south during the cold months. They are the Redwing, and Fieldfare. Both species are gregarious, and are often found in mixed flocks.

Over the grassy uplands Skylarks and Meadow-pipits are very

common, and in walled country one of our earliest migrants may be seen, namely the Wheatear. It will perch on a wall or hillock, being very conspicuous with a smart grey back, warm brown underparts and white rump. Rather smaller in stature than the Wheatear are the Stonechat and Whinchat. These birds both love the heathland. Gorse bushes and dwarf willow make favourite vantage points for these two, and very debonair they are as they sit rather upright. The features that differentiate the two are the black head and white cheeks of the male Stonechat, the white eye stripe and white wing feathers of the Whinchat.

The flocks of Finches always bring a splash of colour. The brilliant little Goldfinches, with broad yellow wing bars, easily identified by their red face, white cheeks and black cap, are often seen feeding on thistles. The handsome Bullfinch with crimson red breast, black cap and white rump is equally distinctive. It has a bad reputation with gardeners and fruit growers, but you are just as likely to see it out in the country feeding on mountain ash, or thorn tree berries. According to statistics Chaffinches are supposed to be one of our commonest birds, and they can also become amazingly tame. Greenfinches are often found in company with the other species, but having a more sombre colouring they do not attract our attention in the same way. The Linnet is another of the smaller Finches, its song being often heard before the bird is spotted. Its chief colour feature is a pinkish red breast. It often favours clumps of gorse, and thick hedges, where in spring a rather frail nest is placed rather low down and well hidden. Of all the Finches the Hawfinch is certainly the most wary and difficult to approach. It is the largest Finch, predominantly brown in colour, with a large bill, and a broad white wing bar. All Finches flock at times, and fly with a strong undulating flight.

One rare bird that is a fairly regular visitor to East Anglia is the Crossbill; it has been known to breed there, and as the name implies it has cross mandibles. The plumage is bright red with darker wings and tail, and it feeds on the seed of conifers.

Of the dozen or more species of Buntings three will readily be found in the area covered by this book. The Yellow Bunting, better known as the Yellow Hammer, is very common, and widely distributed. A near relative, the Cirl Bunting, is comparatively rare, but both are found in similar localities. Along a suitable stream or waterway especially where there is willow and alder we find the Reed Bunting. A rather striking bird, the size of a House Sparrow, it has a black cap and bib with a broad white moustachial stripe extending to the neck and below the bib. A fourth species that is not uncommon in the Salisbury Plain area is the Corn Bunting. It is not very easy to identify being a buff colour, with a rather thickset appearance. In early winter the Snow Bunting will pass across the South Downs on migration. It is a very confident bird and will permit the careful watcher to come within a few feet. In white winter plumage they are unlike any other British bird.

In the vicinity of water the Pied Wagtail, more commonly known as the Water Wagtail, will attract our attention. It will run at a truly astonishing speed for a small bird, and on stopping immediately flicks its long tail up and down. The Grey Wagtail is found in similar localities. It is one of our most lovely and dainty birds, with underparts a beautiful shade of yellow. The Yellow Wagtail which is not so widely distributed may be found in drier pasture land. It is distinguished from the Grey by having a yellow head, shading to olive on the back.

Our common Wren is a resident from sea level to the highest hills, with its perky stance, and scolding chatter accompanying us. The Robin with its confiding nature is well known and loved by all.

From early April until the end of September Britain is home to a vast number of summer migrants. To most people hearing the Cuckoo, and seeing the first Swallow heralds in the spring. At this time many species of Warblers begin to arrive. Identification is difficult as they all appear to look a shade of green, olive, or brown, and seldom remain still long enough to be studied in detail. The Dartford Warbler is the one species of Warbler that, although uncommon, is resident in the southern counties. The varied and fluent songs are the surest means of identification.

Good examples are the Nightingale, Blackcap, and Garden Warbler.

Swallows and Martins are observed hawking for insects, and often fly very close to the ground in warm thundery weather. The two chief distinguishing features are the long outer tail feathers of the Swallow, and the shorter tail and white rump of the Martin. Also along the sand pits of the south we will find colonies of Sand Martins nesting in holes, that they themselves have excavated. They are shorter and more predominantly brown than the House Martins.

In May the scimitar-winged Swift arrives. It spends practically all its time in the air hunting for insects at great heights. It is quite distinctive in black plumage, wheeling and screaming overhead.

Our three species of Woodpeckers are resident with us all year round. The Green Woodpecker or 'Yaffle' is the most frequently seen and heard. Nearly as common is the Great Spotted. This is the one we hear hammering away at a dead tree, the noise of which can be heard over a great distance. A smaller version is the Lesser Spotted. Both the last mentioned are black and white barred on the back and wings, with a red crowned head. Similar in habitat are the Nuthatch and Tree Creeper. Both species are fascinating to watch in their constant search for grubs and other insects lurking in the bark. The Nuthatch has a warm chestnut breast, and underparts, a soft slate grey back, and very short tail. The Tree Creeper is slightly smaller and has a streaky brown back, white underparts and a comparatively long, down-curved bill. The family of tits should also be included with the woodland birds. The common Blue-tits and Great-tits are frequent visitors to the bird tables. The Long-tailed-tits are found usually in family parties, and in certain areas of East Anglia the rare Bearded-tit breeds in the reed beds.

Coots, Moorhens and Grebes are usually seen swimming and feeding in the reed beds of ponds, reservoirs, and the more sluggish streams. The Little Grebe, also known as the Dab-chick, must be one of our quickest divers. It disappears under the water in a flash leaving barely a ripple to mark the spot. As bald as a

L

Coot is an apt description of this bird, a conspicuous white shield appears to extend the bill over the forehead to the crown. The Moorhen's bill is red with a yellow tip, and the white under the tail feathers is very noticeable when the bird is swimming. A bird that frequents haunts similar to the last three is the shy Water Rail. It will seldom take flight, preferring to hide in the reed beds. It has a fairly long bill, and a very short tail.

The rambler will certainly come across game birds, although often the first indication of their presence is a whirr of wings as a hen Pheasant or Partridge is flushed from almost under the walker's feet, so perfectly do these birds blend in with their surroundings. East of Devonshire the Red-legged or French Partridge is well distributed, and appears to prefer dry localities, including the chalk downlands. The smallest of the family is the Quail, only 7in long. It is a migratory bird, and is possessed with a ventriloquial voice. It is more often heard than seen, and then only rarely.

Waders of many species frequent the high downs, reservoirs, marshes, in fact anywhere that food or shelter may be found. The one species of wader that is peculiar to the area covered by this book is the Stone Curlew. It breeds sparingly in Wiltshire, Berkshire and East Anglia, where it is known by a local name of 'Thick knee'. It is nowhere very common, and is identified from other waders by a very short bill, heavy yellow legs and its large size. Lapwings in contrast are found everywhere, at times in immense flocks, especially in autumn and winter. Golden Plovers and Grey Plovers come south to winter with us, but return to the North of England to breed, so that we seldom see these birds in summer plumage. The Oyster-catcher is very common along the coast, but will come inland during hard weather. It is quite distinctive, with black and white plumage, long orange red bill, and pink legs. One of the sounds associated with open spaces is the wild ringing call of the Common Curlew; it is often heard during the night as flocks fly over calling to each other. The nest is just a mere depression on the ground lined with a few dead grasses and is difficult to locate on account of the excellent camouflage of the four large eggs. In the autumn, over damp or marshy ground flushed Snipe cry with a harsh rasping call, and rise rapidly with the characteristic zigzag flight. The quick observer might just see the very long straight bill before the birds wheel out of sight.

During the winter months we have a large increase in the Wood-cock population, which is unfortunate for the birds, as it also coincides with the shooting season. It is a much heavier bird in flight than the Snipe, and is found chiefly in the drier woodlands. Down by the water's edge of the larger rivers, especially where tidal, Redshanks, Ringed Plover and Sand-pipers are desporting themselves in the mud. Later in the year (from August) some of the more spectacular waders come south. These include the Black-tailed Godwit which is almost as large as a Curlew and has a lovely warm chestnut breast and long straight bill, and the Bar-tailed Godwit which is very slightly smaller and is more chestnut in colour, with a slightly upturned bill. Under the care and efforts of the RSPB the lovely Avocet has returned to East Anglia as a breeding species, and during the autumn and winter months, with luck, might be seen in any one of the large river estuaries.

On the edges of streams, ponds, and meres the stately Heron attracts our attention. We are unlikely to confuse this species with any other British bird. It stands 3ft tall, and when in flight its slow deliberate wing beats are also very distinctive. In a similar habitat one might see the brilliant Kingfisher. Described as a jewel amongst birds, it is one of the most vividly coloured of all our birds, but unfortunately is rather uncommon and solitary.

Largely nocturnal in habits, Owls will be more often heard than seen. The beautifully plumaged Barn Owl is becoming rare. When we see it hunting, as it often does at dusk, it looks pre-dominantly white, but closer study shows it to be warm gold and light brown. Tawny owls are the most widely distributed but prefer wooded country or parklands, although farm outbuildings are often chosen as nesting sites. The Little Owl will take up a vantage point on a telegraph post or old building. He looks a dumpy fellow with a flat head, but is very much awake. Somehow

L*

it has acquired a bad reputation for being a predator of smaller birds. The Long-eared Owl and Short-eared Owl are unlikely to be seen when walking, although I do remember once sheltering under a large holly tree, and discovering that I was being watched by a Long-eared Owl.

Birds of prey have a strange fascination. Who, having witnessed the powerful swoop of a Peregrine, can fail to admire the mastery of this falcon? In contrast the broad-winged Buzzard can be seen sailing and soaring on motionless wings over the downs. It has extended its range from the western counties, but is unlikely to be found east of the New Forest. The Kestrel will be the most common bird of prey, often seen hovering, facing into the wind, in the constant search for food. It will suddenly drop like a stone on to some unsuspecting mouse, or beetle. A more dashing hunter is the Sparrow Hawk, shorter of wing than the Kestrel and generally darker, which tends to fly low along hedgerows, where its favourite victim is probably another bird. Salisbury Plain is the haunt of the rare Hobby. It favours the small clumps of trees that dominate the rounded hills. The eggs are often laid in the acquired nest of a Carrion Crow. The plumage is somewhat similar to a Peregrine, with dark head and white under the throat, and it is approximately the size of a Kestrel. On one occasion I was lucky enough to see the lovely male Hen Harrier quartering the heath on the Purbeck Hills. The soft grey mantle and buoyant flight are very distinctive. In East Anglia the rare Marsh Harrier breeds under the watchful eyes of various RSPB wardens. It is a darker bird than the Hen Harrier, but has the same buoyant flight, and is to be found in marshy country and areas of dense reed beds.

The species of duck, geese, and swans, which the walker may see will depend almost entirely on the season of the year and where he is, along the three hundred odd miles of pathway. In Dorset the famous Swannery at Abbotsbury is well known, and well worth a visit. From the loneliest downlands to the city ornamental ponds, Mallard, and Teal are found. The Shelduck also breeds in suitable localities. The flooded gravelpits are a refuge for many species of duck, including Goldeneye, Tufted, Pintail, Wigeon, and the lovely Great Crested Grebe, the latter being distinguished from the ducks by a pointed bill, and dark ear tufts. In the winter, especially near the east coast, vast quantities of duck, and geese arrive. The sight that gladdens the heart of the country lover, is to see these flights come over at dusk or early morning in chevron formation: silhouetted against the cold winter sky and reminiscent of a Peter Scott painting.

Returning to the Isle of Wight area we must mention a few of the sea birds. We shall see Black-headed Gulls most of the year. In the winter the black 'cap' is missing, but the red legs and bill enable us to differentiate between this species and the Kittiwake. The large Herring Gull is common, coming several miles inland to forage for food. The Cormorant and its smaller cousin the Shag will often be found at some distance from the sea, although most of them nest along the cliff.

This by no means exhausts the list, and there are many species of birds we might see that have not been mentioned in this rather condensed appendix.

Bibliography
Campbell, B. and Tinggaard, K. A. *Birds in Colour*, 1960
Campbell, C. and Watson, D. *The Oxford Book of Birds*, 1964
Fisher, J. *The Shell Bird Book*, 1966
Fitter, R. S. R. *Collins Guide to Bird Watching*, 1963
Fitter, R. S. R. and Richardson, R. A. *Collins Pocket Guide to British Birds*, 1966

IV

WILD FLOWERS OF THE CHALK

by Alan Charles

THE same processes which, in relatively late geological time, culminated in the gently rolling contours of chalk downland, have, in their turn, endowed the landscape with a particularly rich and varied community of wild flowers. The warm, well-drained, well-aerated chalk soil is the basis of many of the most attractive British wild flower species.

Wild flowers of the chalk have for many years been the subject of considerable study and research by both professional and amateur botanists; much knowledge and enthusiasm has accumulated as a result. Although the reader may not wish to emulate the botanical expert, his pleasure in walking the chalk downland can be enhanced considerably through no more than an elementary understanding of the flora and its environment. The aim throughout these few paragraphs is to lay the foundation of an understanding without involving the reader in the more complex details of the subject.

It has not been possible to mention more than a few of the wild flowers to be found on chalk soils, and the selection is from those which are most likely to be noticed by the casual observer by reason of their abundance or appearance. The existence of so great a variety of species on the downland of Southern England is largely due to the tolerance which many plants show for this lime-rich medium: a chalk or limestone soil is essential to some species (the 'calcicoles'), strongly preferred by others, tolerated by the remainder. This last group will tolerate a wide range of soils and is consequently represented in many diverse areas—not only on the chalk.

It should be remembered that the chalk is in places overlaid with superficial deposits of sand, gravel or clay where wild flowers not characteristic of chalky soils may be found; the ability to identify various soil types is the first step in avoiding any confusion which may arise.

Unshaded grassland is the largest single chalk downland habitat for wild flowers and one around which most interest has centred. The short turf has been preserved over the centuries by the grazing of sheep and rabbits and sustains an inheritance of flowering plants particularly suited to this delicately balanced environment. Recent years have witnessed a considerable decline in grazing on the downs and an increase in land coming under the plough: many areas are reverting to the natural cycle of plant succession in which the turf gives way to scrub and the scrub to woodland, while others are irretrievably lost to agriculture. It is fortunate that numerous chalk grassland areas are afforded some protection through their status as Nature Reserves or Sites of Special Scientific Interest.

One of the most attractive species to be found on chalk grassland is the common rock rose; when seen in large numbers on a bank or hillside on a sunny day the delicate yellow flowers present a most pleasing aspect. Another species with a preference for chalky soils is the common milkwort, a short tufty plant with pink, white or blue flowers in bloom from May into September.

Five members of the pea family are worthy of mention in view of their interest and abundance: these are the horse-shoe vetch, birdsfoot trefoil, kidney vetch, black medick and the rest harrow. The colourful birdsfoot trefoil grows in a great variety of unshaded habitats, not only on the chalk, and possession of more than seventy local names is evidence of its special status in country lore. Examples are: butter and eggs; boots and shoes; rosy morn; cuckoo's stockings; bunny rabbit's ears. The kidney vetch is not without interest: it has an amazing power of reproduction in that its seeds have been known to germinate after lying dormant for at least ninety years. The black medick is so named from the blackness of its seed pods when ripe; the rest harrow from its antagonism to the ploughman's harrow.

Some plants have virtue added to beauty. The salad burnet was once used for the curing of wounds; it is an acceptable addition to the green salad and is much favoured by downland sheep. The sweetly scented ladies' or yellow bedstraw was used for the curdling of milk in cheesemaking, its stems crushed in the manufacture of red dye, and the whole plant gathered in large quantities as filling for mattresses.

Of the eyebrights there exist about twenty-five species—many of which are difficult to distinguish—with the collective name of *Euphrasia officinalis*. The most attractive of these is the common eyebright and the large-flowered chalk eyebright. The large-flowered eyebright has been described as 'one of the autumn gems of the downs' on account of the magnificence of its September bloom.

Five common members of the daisy family found on chalk grassland are the field and small scabious, the musk and stemless and carline thistles. The large drooping heads of the musk make it one of the most handsome of thistle species. The carline is hardly less attractive; its pale yellow flowers open fully in the sunlight and close when conditions are wet or humid.

Two chalk-loving gentians worth seeking-out are the felwort and the yellow-wort. The reddish-purple flowers of the felwort are very sensitive to temperature: they will open and close at the incredible speed of one minute or less.

Self-heal, wild thyme and marjoram are examples of the dead-nettle family found in some abundance on the downs. As its name suggests, self-heal was in earlier days greatly esteemed for its medicinal properties; wild thyme is particularly noted for the sweetness of its scent; marjoram for its aroma.

For the downland walker few delights compare with the unexpected discovery of a solitary orchid with its attractive head dominating the surrounding vegetation. Two species most likely to be found are the appropriately named fragrant and pyramidal orchids. Examples of less common species are the bee and man orchids and the autumn lady's tresses.

Other examples of common chalk grassland species are: cowslip, plantain, squinancywort, fairy flax, mouse-eared hawkweed, viper's bugloss, centauri and the umbelliferae: wild carrot, wild parsnip, hare's ear and lesser burnet saxifrage.

Next in importance to chalk grassland areas are the shady places such as woodland margins and clearings, hedgebanks and fieldsides. For simplicity these habitats are here gathered under one heading: chalk woodland.

Prominent among chalk woodland flowers during the early days of spring are three species of violet: the wood dog, the hairy and the sweet-scented. The wood dog violet is the most common of the three species and, like the hairy violet, has no scent. The hairy violet is not restricted to woodland but also grows on unshaded chalk grassland. The hairy leaves are a vital factor in the plant's ability to conserve moisture—a useful attribute when growing on dry hillsides.

A versatile woodland plant is the sweet woodruff. This 'herb of cordiality' had a great diversity of uses: it was put in wine; in beds; on floors; and it was common practice to scent the folds of clean linen with the dried leaves. Woodruff tea was said to be delicious.

Among the most admired and sought-after chalk woodland flowers are those orchid species which prefer some degree of shade. The common spotted orchis—orchis being a genus within the orchid family—is very abundant and easily recognised by the dark blotches on its leaves. Another common orchid is the butter-fly, the sweet-scented flowers of which are pollinated by moths. The fly and bird's-nest orchids and certain of the helleborines are examples of species less likely to be found on account of their rarity or local distribution.

Also common among chalk woodland flowers are the attractive wild basil, the sanicle, the common wintergreen and the dog's mercury. The dog's mercury is not particularly outstanding in appearance but does possess a remarkable ability to keep all rivals at bay by sheer weight of numbers.

The wild carrot completes this short woodland survey; as summer days give way to autumn, the delicate flower-heads curve inwards forming a cup-shaped appearance notably similar to the bird's-nest of the hedgerows.

Bibliography

Fitter, R. S. R. *Finding Wild Flowers*, 1971

Louseley, J. E. *Wild Flowers of Chalk and Limestone*, 1969

McClintock, D. and Fitter, R. S. R. *Collins Pocket Guide to Wild Flowers*, 1956

Martin, Keble. *Concise British Flora in Colour*, 1969

Nicholson, B. E., Ary, S. and Gregory, M. *The Oxford Book of Wild Flowers*, 1960 (Pocket Edition, 1970)

Skene, MacGregor. *A Flower Book for the Pocket*, 1952

V

THE EIGHT-HUNDRED-FOOT
CHALK HILLS

1 Walbury Hill 974ft (SU3761) Berks (county summit)
2 Milk Hill 964ft (SU1064) Wilts (joint county summit)
3 Tan Hill 964ft (SU0864) Wilts (joint county summit)
4 Inkpen Hill 954ft (SU3561) Berks
5 Combe Hill 953ft (SU3860) Berks
6 Martinsell Hill 950ft (SU1763) Wilts
7 Long Knoll 944ft (ST7837) Wilts
8 Pilot Hill 937ft (SU3860) Hants (county summit)
9 Brimsdown Hill 933ft (ST8239) Wilts
10 Win Green Hill 910ft (ST9220) Wilts
11 Liddington Castle 910ft (SU2079) Wilts
12 Bulbarrow Hill 901ft (ST7705) Dorset
13 Hackpen Hill—Central summit 892ft (SU1274) Wilts
14 Butser Hill 888ft (SU7120) Hants (highest point of the South
    Downs)
15 Hackpen Hill—South-west summit 887ft (SU1273) Wilts
16 Hackpen Hill—North-east summit 884ft (SU1375) Wilts
17 Golden Ball Hill 879ft (SU1363) Wilts
18 Point 879 (Barbury Castle) 879ft (SU1576) Wilts
19 Botley Hill 875ft (TQ3955) Surrey (highest point of North
    Downs)
20 Wexcombe Down 874ft (SU2757) Wilts
21 Sidown Hill 872ft (SU4457) Hants
22 Telegraph Hill 871ft (ST6404) Dorset
23 Gore Hill 863ft (ST6303) Dorset
24 Melbury Hill 862ft (ST8719) Dorset
25 Point 860 860ft (SU2956) Wilts
26 Charlton Down 859ft (ST8920) Dorset
27 Beacon Hill 858ft (SU4557) Hants
28 Knap Hill 857ft (SU1263) Wilts

29 Point 857 857ft (SP8908) Bucks (county summit and highest point of the Chilterns)
30 Huish Hill 856ft (SU1563) Wilts
31 Whitehorse Hill 856ft (SU3086) Berks
32 Nettlecombe Tout 855ft (ST7302) Dorset
33 Point 855 855ft (ST6703) Dorset
34 Morgan's Hill 853ft (SU0366) Wilts
35 Point 852 852ft (SU4059) Hants
36 Cherhill Down 852ft (SU0569) Wilts
37 Aston Hill 852ft (SP8909) Bucks
38 Whitefield Hill 850+ft (SU2176) Wilts
39 Point 850+ 850+ft (TQ4055) Surrey
40 Haydown Hill 845ft (SU3156) Wilts
41 Cold Kitchen Hill 845ft (ST8438) Wilts
42 Coombe Hill 842ft (SP8406) Bucks
43 Point 839 839ft (ST9320) Wilts
44 Littleton Down (Tegleaze) 836ft (SU9415) Sussex
45 Shirburn Hill 835ft (SU7295) Oxon (county summit)
46 Charlbury Hill 829ft (SU2382) Wilts
47 Eggardon Hill 827ft (SY5494) Dorset
48 Ball Hill 825ft (ST7203) Dorset
49 Betsom's Hill 824ft (TQ4356) Kent (county summit)
50 Little Down 823ft (SU3055) Wilts
51 Bell Hill 818ft (ST8007) Dorset
52 Point 816 816ft (SP9615) Bucks
53 Linch Down 814ft (SU8417) Sussex
54 Ditchling Beacon 813ft (TQ3313) Sussex
55 Wheatham Hill 813ft (SU7427) Hants
56 Pulpit Hill 813ft (SP8305) Bucks
57 Batcombe Hill 812ft (ST6103) Dorset
58 Point 811 811ft (SP8203) Bucks
59 Point 810 810ft (ST8918) Dorset
60 Toller Down 810ft (ST5202) Dorset
61 Warren Corner 808ft (SU7227) Hants
62 Crowell Hill 806ft (SU7599) Oxon
63 Burton Down 803ft (SU9613) Sussex

64 White Sheet Hill 802ft (ST8034) Wilts
65 Point 802 802ft (SP9109) Herts (county summit)
66 Point 801 801ft (SU7219) Hants
67 Beaminster Down 800ft (ST4903) Dorset
68 Wain Hill 800+ft (SP7700) Bucks

Note

The qualification for inclusion in the above list is at least one separate contour ring of 800ft or above on the 1 inch O.S. Map; it could perhaps be contended that two separate contour rings would provide a more satisfactory criterion. Named hills with no contour rings are classified as shoulders of higher hills and not included.

VI

THE PRESENT STATE OF THE
OFFICIAL PATHS

North Downs Way

The section from Dover to Hollingbourne by way of Canterbury is complete. It is effectively waymarked and has been officially opened. The alternative route from Dover lacks rights-of-way in several places between there and Stowting and a way has to be made on existing roads or public footpaths.

Hollingbourne to Thurnham Castle—the exact details of the route are still under consideration, but alternatives are available.

New road schemes around Wrotham may enforce alterations to the line in the not too distant future.

West Yaldham to Otford—the exact details of the route are still under negotiation; alternatives are available.

From Tatsfield to A22, while the general line is settled and can be followed, the precise line is still under negotiation.

In Square 1550 (near Dorking) the exact route has not yet been settled, but there are acceptable alternatives nearby.

The footbridge across the River Wey below Guildford is not yet available, enforcing a detour by a footbridge nearer the town.

South Downs Way

This is complete, waymarked (stone plinths in East Sussex, wooden arms in West Sussex) and has been officially opened.

The bridge over the River Adur should become available during 1974, after which the detour by Bramber and Steyning will no longer be necessary.

Truleigh Hill Hostel should be available during 1974.

Ridgeway Path

This is almost complete, is being waymarked and will be opened officially late in 1973.

186

However, negotiation is still in progress over the exact line at the following points:

(a) the railway crossing at Tring

(b) Tring Park

(c) in the neighbourhood of Hastoe village

(d) between Coombe Hill, Wendover and Buckmoorend

(e) crossing the park at Chequers.

Projected trunk road developments near Tring may also enforce changes in the line in the future.

No other route in this book is presented as a continuous long-distance right-of-way and the walker on other ridgeways must travel under the guidance of the 1 inch O.S. Map (which in the latest editions indicates rights-of-way), modified by such notices as he encounters along the way. When there are no path lines in the right direction, minor roads and lanes still give pleasant going in many parts of our area and long-distance walks of great charm can be strung together at will.

GENERAL BIBLIOGRAPHY

Beckinsale, R. P. *Companion into Berkshire*, Bourne End, 1972

Belloc, H. *The Old Road*, 1904

Camp, J. *Portrait of Buckinghamshire*, 1972

Cheetham, J. H. and Piper, J. *Wiltshire—Shell Guide*, 1968

Cracknell, B. *Portrait of Surrey*, 1970

Crouch, M. *Kent*, 1966

Darton, F. J. Harvey. *The Marches of Wessex*, 1936

Dickson, Annan. *Portrait of the Chilterns*, 1971

Dorman, B. E. *Norfolk*, 1972

Dutton, R. *Hampshire*, 1970

Eastbourne Rambling Club. *Along the South Downs*, 1973

Fairfax-Blakeborough, J. *Yorkshire—East Riding*, 1951

FitzGerald, K. *The Chilterns*, 1972

Good, R. *The Old Roads of Dorset*, Dorchester, 1940

Goodsall, R. H. *The Ancient Road to Canterbury*, 1960

Green, E. G. *The South Downs Way*, 1968

Harper, C. G. *The Dorset Coast*, 1905

Harper, C. G. and Kershaw, J. C. *The Downs and the Sea*, 1923

Harrison, D. *Along the South Downs*, 1958

Harrod, H. and Linnell, C. L. S. *Norfolk*, 1957

Higham, R. *The South Country*, 1972

Hoskins, W. G. *The Making of the English Landscape*, 1957

Hughes, P. *Isle of Wight—Shell Guide*, 1967

——. *Kent—Shell Guide*, 1969

Hughes, T. *The Scouring of the White Horse*, 1859

Hyams, J. *Dorset*, 1970

Jennett, S. *The Pilgrims' Way*, 1971

Massingham, H. J. *Chiltern Country*, 1940

——. *English Downland*, 1936, 1949

Maxwell, D. *The Pilgrims' Way to Kent*, 1932

Pitt-Rivers, M. *Dorset—Shell Guide*, 1966

Pridham, L. *The Dorset Coastline*, Dorchester, nd

Pyatt, E. C. *Climbing and Walking in South-East England*, Newton Abbot, 1970

Rubinstein, D. *The Wolds Way*, Clapham, Yorks, 1972

Short, B. C. *The Isle of Purbeck*, 1967

Street, P. *Portrait of Wiltshire*, 1971

Thomas, Edward. *The Icknield Way*, 1913

Timperley, H. W. *The Vale of Pewsey*, 1954

White, Gilbert. *The Natural History of Selborne*, 1789 (and many later editions)

Whitlock, R. *Salisbury Plain*, 1955

Wightman, R. *Portrait of Dorset*, 1965

Willard, B. *Sussex*, 1965

Wilson, L. *Portrait of the Isle of Wight*, 1965

Wooldridge, S. W. and Goldring, F. *The Weald*, 1953

Wooldridge, S. W. and Hutchings, G. E. *London's Countryside*, 1964

Wright, C. J. *A Guide to the Pilgrims' Way and the North Downs Way*, 1971

Wyndham, R. *South East England*, 1951

ACKNOWLEDGEMENTS

THE origins of this book go back to before the days of official long-distance footpaths, before the days of highly efficient personal transport, when the nearer chalk ridgeways were the Londoner's only attainable walking country for days and weekends. It owes much to many people who walked and talked with me then, and to others down the years to the present day. We have seen the roads so changed by the increase in car traffic as to be almost unusable by the foot traveller. Fortunately the rise in status and state of preservation of footpaths has broadly retained the access to the countryside, which we then enjoyed, in a different but certainly equally acceptable form.

I should like to thank the following for help in various ways: Cyril Manning and Alan Charles for appendices on 'Birds' and 'Flowers' respectively; Paul Sharp; Miss P. M. Lutgen and Messrs R. F. Brown, V. D. Ellis, S. P. Taylor and C. T. Williams of the Countryside Commission for copious information and helpful criticism; the Libraries of the Alpine Club and of the Borough of Richmond upon Thames; J. Allan Cash, Ronald Clark, Leslie and Marjorie Gayton and Aerofilms Ltd for photographs; the Defence Land Agent for information on paths on Salisbury Plain; the Hampshire County Land Agent; the Ordnance Survey for data on which the maps were based.

My wife has given, as always, help and encouragement at all stages, and my daughter, Gillian, has undertaken the main responsibility for the maps.

Hampton   Edward C. Pyatt